I Never Worked a Day in My Life

The Service Merchandise Story

T0266496

I Never Worked a Day in My Life

The *Service* Merchandise Story

A Half Century Building a
Retail Dream Together

RAYMOND ZIMMERMAN

Advantage | Books

Published by Advantage, Charleston, South Carolina.
Member of Advantage Media.

ADVANTAGE is a registered trademark, and the Advantage colophon is a trademark of Advantage Media Group, Inc.

Printed in the United States of America.

10 9 8 7 6 5 4 3 2 1

ISBN: 978-1-64225-284-2 (Paperback)
ISBN: 978-1-64225-433-4 (eBook)

LCCN: 2022913402

Cover design by Hampton Lamoureux.
Layout design by Amanda Haskin.

This publication is designed to provide accurate and authoritative information in regard to the subject matter covered. It is sold with the understanding that the publisher is not engaged in rendering legal, accounting, or other professional services. If legal advice or other expert assistance is required, the services of a competent professional person should be sought.

Advantage Media helps busy entrepreneurs, CEOs, and leaders write and publish a book to grow their business and become the authority in their field. Advantage authors comprise an exclusive community of industry professionals, idea-makers, and thought leaders. Do you have a book idea or manuscript for consideration? We would love to hear from you at **AdvantageMedia.com**.

CONTENTS

ACKNOWLEDGMENTS

I am deeply grateful to the many people, past and present, without whom this book could not have been.

Thank you to my loving parents, sisters, grandparents, aunts, uncles, and cousins for their devotion and guidance. Thank you to our children and their families and all the grandchildren for their love, encouragement, and assistance. Thank you to the loyal and grounded friends who have enriched my life immeasurably.

Thank you to the hundreds of thousands of wonderful people who worked so hard at Service Merchandise to make it a great company—and a great family. Thank you to all the vendors, suppliers, and bankers who believed in us and kept us going, through good times and bad.

Thank you to the millions and millions of customers who shopped with us. I hope that we served you well and that you thoroughly enjoyed your purchases.

Thank you to all those who helped me at my publisher, Advantage Media|Forbes Books, and particularly my writing partner, Bob, who was with me every word of the way.

And a huge thank you to Etta—my wife, my honeylove, best friend, partner. Without you, I would have been long gone. Though

I wasn't always easy to handle, you stood by me, for better and for worse, in sickness and in health. I love you all the world, and then some. Thank you for our twenty-eight fabulous years, and here's to twenty-eight more.

To each and all of you, I send my love.

INTRODUCTION: THE MERCHANTS OF MEMORIES

"We may have sold 'things,' but we were really merchants of memories. We provided the backdrop upon which families crafted cherished remembrances and filled scrapbooks."

Rob Mitchell, former Service Merchandise associate, as posted on Facebook

My father holds my hand as the midnight train pulls into our little town of Pulaski, Tennessee. We step into the club car, where I curl up at his side, lulled to sleep by the murmur of voices and rhythms from the track. He is talking with other men in the car—men like him, store owners from small towns and cities along the way, heading to the annual New York City Toy Fair to see the latest offerings on the market. It is 1941, and I am eight years old, and all I know is that I am with a good man, and we will see the big city together—and, yes, toys will be involved.

We will go on many more such journeys in the years ahead, to Chicago and other destinations where buyers and sellers convene,

1

and I will grow ever taller and tuned in to the ways of the business world. "Get to know people and make friends, Raymond," I recall my father telling me. "They'll trust you and take care of you." It is one of many lessons this wise man will teach me through the years. None of those other trips, though, will match the anticipation of this weekend together. We are on our way to wonderland.

"Let's go!" my father says, smiling broadly, after we have settled into our hotel room for some rest. He guides me along the bustling Manhattan sidewalks to a display window of the Woolworths store on Thirty-Fourth Street, where I behold a profusion of toys beyond my imagination. "And you'll see these again at the toy show, Son," he says. "See, this is where the vendors test whether the new lines will sell." More of his grown-up talk. I'm just wishing I could crawl inside the window to play.

"Daddy," I exclaim, my eyes fixed on the display, "we need to get us a store like this one!" I look up at him. "This must be the biggest five-and-ten in the whole wide world!"

Fast-forward to 1978, and I am standing there again, my son at my side, hoping to find again that window of delight. Let's just say that the place isn't quite the same, that standards have slipped. "So this is the great store we came all the way here to see?" a puzzled Freddy, then twelve, asks me, and I sigh. My thoughts are wistful: *When I was a kid, this was such a marvelous preview to the toy show. Why must everything change?*

"Well, then, let's go buy your bar mitzvah suit!" I tell my son, and we make the most of our weekend. In those days I traveled to New York and other cities a lot, often with Freddy or my daughter, Robyn, and sometimes their friends. Yes, so much had changed—and now we were building new memories, gathering new souvenirs of our time together.

All my days, come what may, I will cherish that long-ago weekend with my father. Eight decades later, I can close my eyes and still see every line of his face as he grins at me. It still is vivid, as are so many other scenes from a boyhood and a manhood spent striving toward something better.

Think of this book as a love letter to the Service Merchandise family—to those many souls across the nation who were employed with us, shopped with us, did business with us, or helped us raise money for philanthropy. This book is a collection of memories, as best as I can recall them, built upon the timeline of who we were, on the way to what we have become. It is a series of snapshots of an American century. Whether you and I have met or not, we are friends nonetheless in that we put our hearts in the same place. I write this book so that we might always be together.

Come with me now on a journey through time—from our beginnings in 1934 as a five-and-ten-cent store, our transition to wholesale, and our evolution into a thriving nationwide chain of catalog showrooms that continued into the new millennium. Service Merchandise was more than a store, though we had many of them. We were a family, some of us related by blood but all of us related by mission. Together we spent long hours making things happen. Together we met the ever-changing challenges of the retail business with grace, style, and warmth. And didn't we have us some fun!

Let me introduce myself: I am Raymond Zimmerman, and for decades I stood proudly at the helm of our enterprise. My career began behind the counter of my family's modest store in that tiny Tennessee town. I had to stand on a box to reach the cash register, but I knew even then that I wanted to be part of a long line of merchants in our family.

As I look back, I am pleased to say that I never worked a day in my life. I labored at times, but it was a labor of love. I had my share of difficulties, but through it all I knew that we were building something—and that's not work. That, my friends, is joy.

It's 1934 ...

- The Great Depression continues to dash dreams.

- Germany and Poland sign a nonaggression pact as global tensions grow.

- Gable and Colbert pack theaters with *It Happened One Night*.

- With Prohibition over, liquor taxes help pay for Roosevelt's New Deal.

- A gallon of gas in the US costs a dime; a Studebaker costs $625.

    ... and in Pulaski, Tennessee, Harry and Mary Zimmerman open a five-and-ten.

Through the Years ...

- 1934: Harry and Mary Krivcher Zimmerman, with baby Raymond, open a Ben Franklin five-and-ten in Pulaski, Tennessee. They soon leave the franchise. Eventually the business expands to a chain of ten stores.

- 1943: Harry is called to military service. After he returns three years later, the family relocates to Nashville.

- 1947: The business begins transitioning from retail into a wholesale operation.

- 1948: The business adds a subsidiary called Service Wholesale that sells housewares in grocery stores.

CHAPTER 1

The Early Years, 1934–1950

MY PARENTS trusted me—so much so that they kept a crate by the cash register of our five-and-ten so that I could climb up to collect my week's pay each Saturday, leaving a slip stating the amount. I was entitled to a quarter, which was enough to see a double-feature Western and fill up on popcorn and procure all else that an eight-year-old boy deemed essential.

On one such payday, I decided that I deserved an extra dime, and I knew just where to get it. I couldn't take it from the cash register—they'd notice! But I had spied a dime hiding in a muffin tin behind the bulk-candy case. My parents had used the tin to sort coins until they could afford the register. The overlooked dime had been calling to me to set it free.

I tried to do the deed stealthily. Scanning the room, I slipped a hand behind the candy case to feel for the muffin tin—and those pilfering fingers encountered instead the spinning blades of a large metal fan that kept away the flies.

My mother heard me yelp. "Raymond! Are you all right?" she called and in a moment was at my side. I tried to hide the evidence behind my back. "Give me your hand," she demanded, grabbing a bandage from the shelves.

My father appeared next and knelt to assist. "What happened here?" he asked me.

"I don't know."

They might have guessed, or I might have confessed, but the truth came out.

"So you wanted more money, Son?" my father asked, looking more sad than angry. "And it was worth this? Why didn't you just tell us what you wanted?"

"I don't know."

I believe, looking back eighty years, that I was telling the truth. I didn't know what had possessed me to do such a thing. But I did feel something far more painful than my bleeding hand. I had disappointed my family. They didn't punish me further. The look in their eyes was enough. And, wonder of wonders, they continued to trust me. They still welcomed my assistance in the store. They encouraged me to keep on keeping on. And that is what impressed me most of all.

Today, I still have a scar on my right index finger to remind me of that morning when I tried to help myself to an undeserved dime. And I have something else. In my heart, I carry a lesson about honesty and trust that has stayed with me for life.

Business in the Bloodline

My parents, Harry and Mary Zimmerman, opened that little five-and-ten in Pulaski, Tennessee, in 1934, not long after my birth. They were pretty much kids themselves, in their early twenties. My father had been working as a life-insurance salesman in the Memphis area, where they had been living with my grandparents. Eager to strike out on their own, they were intrigued with the idea of running their own business—and for good reason. Their parents had started businesses too. Business was in their bloodline.

My grandparents on both sides—Abe and Rae Zimmerman, and Joseph and Annie Krivcher—immigrated from czarist Russia in the 1890s, probably to escape the pogroms, or the threat of them, though I never heard them speak of that widespread persecution. Seeking a better life in America, they came to Memphis. Abe Zimmerman opened a dry goods store. Joseph Krivcher started as a dress manufacturer, then opened a grocery and, later, a furniture store.

Why Memphis? A lot of the Jewish immigrants in the great wave from Eastern Europe settled in destinations such as Tennessee and Texas and along the Mississippi, far from New York City. The established Jews in New York mostly had western European roots. When cultures collide, the differences often turn into distances.

My father, Harry, came into the world in 1911 and was raised as an Orthodox Jew. When he was in his late teens, the B'nai B'rith Youth Organization was planning an international gathering in Memphis, with attendees from far and wide. One of the young people who was helping to organize social events was Mary Krivcher, who began setting up "dates" for the attendees.

Harry Zimmerman happened to be among those whom Mary called seeking volunteers. He had seen her around and had noticed her—but because she had been raised as a Reform Jew, their circles seldom coincided. She called him at random to ask for his assistance.

"Hello, this is Mary Krivcher, and I'm helping with B'nai B'rith. Would you be interested in escorting Miss Sarah Fisher from Milwaukee while she is here?" Mary asked Harry.

"No," Harry told Mary.

"Oh?"

"That's right," said Harry. "I'm not interested in taking her out." He paused just long enough for effect. "But I'll take *you* out."

And so began their romance. Mary lived with her parents several miles outside of town, and Harry would walk that distance every Friday night to court her and then walk back home. Every step was destiny—he wanted no one else, and she considered no other suitor.

A few years later, in 1931, they married and lived, for a time, with her parents. It was a devotion that would endure well over half a century. In all their years together as partners in life and business, I never heard a cross word between them.

A Place of Their Own

Two years after they married, I came along. I was still a toddler when they set out one morning to drive more than two hundred miles eastward from Memphis to spend a few days with two cousins who operated five-and-ten stores in Lewisburg and Fayetteville. There my parents got a close-up look at how well a merchant's income might support their household of three—or four, perhaps, and more. They would be blessed, in years to come, with my two little sisters: Doris, born eight years after me, and Sue, five years after that. Confident that their family would grow, God willing, they wanted a place of their own. They wanted to find their own way in the world and together build a family, a career, a life.

"There's an empty building in Pulaski that could be just right for you," one of the cousins mentioned. "You might be interested in checking it out. It's about thirty miles from here." They were interested, all right. On the way back to Memphis, they headed to that central Tennessee town to see what the future might hold for them there.

As they approached Pulaski, my parents passed what seemed like miles of white fences around the magnificent grounds of the Milky Way Farm, newly established by the Mars candy family. They saw factories and processing plants, among them the Pulaski Pure Milk Company and the General Shoe Company. Arriving in the town, they saw blocks of Victorian houses and an assortment of businesses. Pulaski was home, in those Depression years, to about five thousand people, a mix of Black and White with eight Jewish families. They took note of their potential competition: on the town square was Kuhn's five-and-ten, and on another corner was Reeves Drug Store.

The daylight was starting to fade as they pulled up to the empty storefront on First Street, but they could see clearly what they would be getting. The place wasn't exactly spacious. It was just sixteen feet wide by forty-eight feet deep, with a second floor and a basement. It was built on a hill, and so the basement entrance and the storefront were both at street level. Walking around the lot, they wiped at the windows to peer inside, already imagining how they would use the space, and when their eyes met, they both smiled. This was it. They wasted no time getting in touch with the landlord, and as they headed back to Memphis, they had a lease in hand.

"We've made a big decision," my father announced to my grandparents the next morning. "We're moving to Pulaski …" Even before he could explain, they were groaning. He might not have expected cheers, but he did get tears. My parents didn't doubt that the family wished them well. They didn't doubt that my grandparents would help as much as they could to get them started in business.

"But that's so far!" my grandmother said. "Will we still be seeing much of you?"

"Of course!" Daddy reassured her with a hug. "You'll see plenty of us." Nice words, but Tennessee is a mighty wide state, about six hundred miles from the southwest to northeast corners, and to be separated by even a third of that distance means seeing less of loved ones. I suspect the tears were mostly over me. I was the first grandson, after all, and for seventeen years I would be the only grandson on either side of the family. Grown-ups don't change all that much if you miss seeing them for months on end. But a baby? A baby's season is short. I should know. Today I have four grandsons. The youngest is one year old, as I write this. The oldest is now twenty-five. But wasn't it yesterday that he, too, was tiny?

Through a Child's Eyes

Those early years in Pulaski are forever part of me. I am a man who has had the opportunity to see so many places, but my first impressions of life were in that community and in that store. As my mother and father attended to grown-up matters, I rode my bike through the streets and countryside and played with my friends and got into my share of trouble. And I started my schooling there, in what once had been a hospital in the Civil War. I skipped first grade and went directly to second because the first grade had too many pupils.

Early on, I started helping around the store. I saw the world through a child's eyes. Though the store offered an assortment of sundries, my memories of those years are populated with toys and candy—with scooters and wagons and tricycles, with lemon drops and candy peanuts and chocolate-covered raisins. I became the official toy tester. My job was to play with the toys in front of the store to tantalize the neighborhood kids. In my mind's eye, I see myself at age six wearing white leather holsters and a six-shooter on each hip. I see myself so seriously explaining how to spin a top just right.

When I was old enough, I got the additional duty (which I generously shared with my friends) of assembling the larger toys for sale, the ones that cost all of a dollar, the highest price in the store. On summer afternoons we would gather on the second floor and keep busy, except when we didn't. One day we consulted and decided it would be a good idea to feast on an entire box from a shipment of Goo Goo Clusters—a delightful confection of chocolate, caramel, marshmallow, and peanuts—and that same day I had the less than delightful experience of getting my stomach pumped at the hospital.

The shopkeeper's world was the one I knew. I imagined myself in that role when I grew up someday, though I hadn't a clue about the nuts and bolts of running a business. That's what parents were for. They were determined to make this venture succeed. Even as a little boy, I felt honored that they would want me to help around the store. They were demonstrating to me that by taking care of business, they were taking care of me. To do that, they needed to make money—and that meant, above all, caring for the customers. That much I could see. More for them didn't mean less for me.

The Pulaski store opened as a franchise in the Ben Franklin chain of five-and-tens. Under the arrangement, my parents were expected to purchase virtually all their goods from warehouses operated by the Butler Brothers, the franchisor and wholesaler.

"With this store, you can expect to do $8,000 of business a year," a Butler Brothers representative told them as they were getting ready to open the doors. That seemed like plenty for a place that mostly would be bringing in nickels and dimes. During that first year, however, those nickels and dimes and occasional dollars poured in, and they ended with $12,000 in revenue. They were young, but they were eager to learn and clearly were doing something right. They had what it took to keep the customers coming back.

That franchise arrangement lasted only a few years. My father had added a line of rugs that weren't from the Butler Brothers inventory, and they were selling well. "Get them out of here!" a supervisor insisted when he stopped by the store one day. "That's a violation of your contract." Long story short: The Ben Franklin store became Zimmerman's Five and Ten. The cousins in Fayetteville and Lewisburg, who also had been running Ben Franklin stores, likewise gave up their franchises about the same time.

By 1938, my father was looking at expansion, and his aspirations went well beyond Pulaski. He partnered with the Fayetteville cousin to purchase two stores in west Tennessee, and they added the operator of those stores as a third partner. Meanwhile, the other cousin began buying stores on his own.

My father and his partners decided in 1939 to start a wholesale business, establishing it in Union City and adding a fourth partner there to operate it. Rite Merchandising Company became the first cost-plus wholesaler in the country, selling at cost plus 10 percent. Within a few years, that fourth partner bought out the interests of my father and the others, who returned to managing their retail stores.

Rite Merchandising would go on to serve numerous small businesses in the years ahead—including a young fellow who had opened a store called Walton's Five-and-Ten in Arkansas and was assembling his own collection of Ben Franklin franchises. His name was Sam Walton, who by the time he died in 1992 had grown Walmart into the largest retail chain in the United States. In his autobiography *Sam Walton: Made in America*, Walton wrote about those early days when he often would visit Rite Merchandising:

> I was always looking for offbeat suppliers or sources. I started driving over to Tennessee to some fellows I found who would give me special buys at prices way below what Ben Franklin was charging me.... I'd work in the store all day, then take off around closing and drive that windy road over to the Mississippi River ferry at Cottonwood Point, Missouri, and then into Tennessee with an old homemade trailer hitched to my car. I'd stuff that car and trailer with whatever I could get good deals on.[1]

After leaving the wholesale business, my father and his partners continued to buy their merchandise from Rite for a while—and then, on December 7, 1941, Japanese bombers attacked Pearl Harbor. With the war years in full force, the government issued a slate of constraints on life and commerce. One of the bureaucratic overseers was the Office of Price Administration, which was established to control prices and regulate rationing. Among its decrees: A wholesaler cannot raise prices on old customers, only on new ones. The results were predictable. Rite no longer was supplying to my father and his partners. The company was catering to new customers who would pay more.

In those days of war shortages and ration stamps, it seemed that stores could sell whatever they could get—if they could get it. It took some creativity to keep our shelves stocked. The Fayetteville cousin struck a deal with an acquaintance at the nearby Camp Forrest in Tullahoma, one of the Army's largest training bases at the time, to buy

---

1   Sam Walton, *Sam Walton: Made in America* (New York: Doubleday, June 1992), 31–32.

any excess merchandise from the PX stores, whatever was available. He then would divvy up the goods with my father. And what was available one day was a truckload of Hershey's almond bars. The cousin bought the whole truckload and proudly displayed his share in his large store window on the Fayetteville town square. Candy was hard to come by, and getting this stash was quite a coup. And then the summer sun came out. Chocolate bars don't fare very well in a hot store window. No matter. He broke the molten mess into chunks and sold it all.

I was still so young then, just getting into my double digits. I was aware that times had been tough for so many people, and I'd heard the talk of the big war going on somewhere over there, but I was blessed to have my boyhood and my innocence. Soon enough, the war would touch my family. For now, the seasons passed sweetly. In the summers, we had an ice cream cooler in front of the store—Mother was deft at curling each scoop to make it seem larger—and in the wintertime, we had a popcorn machine. The storefront of Zimmerman's Five and Ten became a popular spot. I felt as if we were the center of the community.

Chocolate bars don't fare very well in a hot store window. No matter. He broke the molten mess into chunks and sold it all.

I was oblivious to the brooding racial tensions of the time. I played with everyone, Black and White, and the fact that we had separate schools and separate water fountains—well, I didn't wonder much about it then. Nor had it occurred to me yet that something was very wrong with the fact that my Black playmates had to make do with textbooks that the White schools deemed too tattered to use anymore. What I did know was we were buddies, the bunch of us, and we would range around town, our laughter echoing in the evening air. I felt secure and accepted growing up in Pulaski. I would have wished that feeling for all my young friends.

AN ANTIDOTE TO RACISM

A footnote on history here: Yes, my hometown of Pulaski, Tennessee, was the birthplace of the Ku Klux Klan (KKK) after the Civil War. And, no, the people of Pulaski are not hateful and intolerant. Quite the contrary.

When I was a boy, we used to play near the building where the KKK founders had met. A plaque on the building pointed it out. Starting in the 1980s, the Klan began holding rallies in Pulaski, trying to capitalize on the birthplace distinction.

Disgusted, the new owner of the building decided to have the plaque dismantled—and then remounted backward, with the inscription against the brick. It served as a call for the good people of Pulaski to turn their back on racism.

And they did. During the next Klan rally, businesses for miles around closed for the day. Hotels and restaurants shut down. The Klansmen came but couldn't find anywhere to eat or to buy gas or even to use a toilet. That kind of quiet solidarity has a way of unraveling a rally. When nobody is paying attention, what's the point of a march?

The five-and-tens that my parents and cousins operated in those Tennessee towns helped keep us in touch. We were a close family—and those stores kept us closer. We lived amid the rhythms of a shopkeeper's day. On Saturdays, after closing time, my parents often would drive to Fayetteville to see our cousins, or our cousins would come to Pulaski. Long past midnight, as I lay awake in bed, I could hear the murmur of the men as they played poker, six guys laughing around a table, their cigar smoke hanging in the air. It all felt so right, because we were together, and we had dreams. In those days I learned some of the first and enduring lessons of life. I was observing, day by day, what a thriving business could do for a family—and how much of a family a business could be.

Where the Love Starts

"Don't go shooting birds, boys!" Dr. Johnson, who lived across the street from us, cried out as he marched over to our backyard one Friday afternoon. Scowling at me and my best friend, he pointed down at the dead robin lying among the fallen leaves. "That little creature didn't do anything but look pretty."

I'm going to say it was Johnny Sharp, the mayor's son, who had taken the lethal aim with his Red Ryder BB gun, though I was likewise armed. Johnny spent a lot of time at my house, and I at his. We were tight as ticks, the two of us, though quite different. He was a natural athlete. I was the fat kid.

And now both of us were killers, in the eyes of the good doctor who had come to lecture us. We bowed our heads, shuffled some, and looked appropriately ashamed until he threw his hands in the air and departed.

"So what now, Raymond?" Johnny asked me.

"Guess it's time for the funeral." It seemed only fitting.

We dug a small hole and placed the robin into it. Then one of us—and I'm going to say it was Johnny—proposed that instead of a burial, we should perform a cremation. We gathered twigs and dry leaves and branches, piled them atop the bird, and set a match to the funeral pyre, standing back to watch our handiwork.

And then the wind picked up. Bordering our backyard was the Pulaski Cemetery, where the grass was crisp that fall from a dry spell. It would soon get crisper. Within minutes the grounds were ablaze. The town firefighters rushed to the scene and trained a hose on the cemetery, drenching it. By then it wasn't just Johnny and me standing back to watch. Quite a crowd had gathered, already whispering theories on what might have led to this. We were looking mighty guilty—and this was going to be a hard one to explain. *See, we were just burning a bird, and, well, all of a sudden this happens. Go figure!*

When it was over, most of the cemetery was charred and sodden. The gravestones were blackened. Plastic flowers at their base had melted. And Johnny and I were in deep trouble. Not only had we courted calamity, but my mother and father had been forced to leave their store on a busy Friday afternoon. And why? Because their boy decided to set the town on fire? It didn't go over too well. And I'm sure Johnny's parents didn't consider his behavior to be exemplary for the son of a mayor and the scion of the town's Ford dealer.

The whole fuss blew over, and we lived to talk about it. I don't know about Johnny, but I didn't get a switching, which is how a lot of parents would have dealt with such a transgression. It wasn't my rear that hurt. It was my ears. My parents took turns making sure that I heard, loud and clear, their disappointments and their expectations of me. My mother was more the disciplinarian, and she could wither me with a look. Every time I would come home past my curfew, she would be waiting—and she might have beat me with a stick, and it wouldn't have hurt as much as that look. It was all the more painful because I knew her to be kindhearted.

They were quite different, my mother and father, and yet each made an indelible impression on me. Both were outgoing, though not overly so—certainly not shy. They made friends easily. They greeted the customers by their first names. They were driven and ambitious, yet laid back too. On slow afternoons, Daddy would retire across the street to play dominoes at the tailor's shop. As a team they were determined to accomplish what they set out to do, each contributing their inner gifts to the outcome.

Though my father made the business and strategy decisions, my mother played a central role in running our store and all the stores that the family would come to operate. Her default mode was one of love and caring, but she could be tough. She made sure that the hired help, and that included me, performed as expected. She demanded a strong work ethic. No high heels, for example. "You can't work if you wear them," she insisted. And if she saw you with your hands in your pockets, you clearly weren't working, and she might very well send you home. Mother was big on compassion but understood that true caring includes correcting and, when necessary, dismissing. As I observed her in action, I came to see what it would take to become a strong manager.

Something about Mary Zimmerman drew others to confide in her. She always seemed to have the inside story on what people were going through, though she wasn't a gossip. They returned to her the affection that they felt from her. They trusted her with their confidences.

As my mom, she wanted to allot me some of the freedoms that every kid covets, but within reason. When I was seven years old, I extracted from her what I believed was a promise that I could start biking around town upon turning eight—but she had second thoughts as she pictured me pedaling along busy Route 64. On my birthday, I shot out of bed, ran to my bicycle, and—

The tires were flat. She had let out the air. I considered what she did that day to be mean. I see it now as loving.

My father, a short and stocky man, seemed to me to know everything about everything, and he was generous and charitable by nature. The table was always full at his card games. I can picture him even now, puffing on a Roi-Tan cigar as he leans back and shuffles the deck.

I remember rushing home from school whenever Daddy promised to take me fishing, and he was good to his word. As he taught me how and where to cast a line, he also taught me how to get along in life. In the years ahead, he would teach me how to pursue and seal a deal—or walk away from one if need be. He was a natural as a father, bigger than life to a little boy looking up to him—and that

I did deeply respect my parents. They believed in second chances, and they shaped who I would become.

child, as he grew to manhood, never ceased wanting his guidance. To this day, as I cast my line into other waters, I still do.

Though I didn't always show it so well in those days, I did deeply respect my parents. They believed in second chances, and they shaped who I would become. Young people need devoted parents because that's where the love starts. "Never go to bed angry," my mother would say, and that refrain became crucially important in the decades ahead as we continued working side by side in bigger stores, many of them, in towns and cities across the land. We would often disagree, but never would anything divide us.

Strategic Moves

In 1944, Daddy was called up for military service, among the last group of fathers to be drafted in World War II. I kissed him goodbye in the Pulaski public square as he joined a few other men on a bus to Nashville and onward to eight weeks of basic training for the Navy. I was eleven, and he was thirty-three, and the family could only hope that the war would soon be winding down.

Stationed at first in Maryland, he soon was deployed to the Philippines for the duration of the war. In his absence, my mother took me and my little sister Doris back to Memphis to live with my grandparents again, leaving the stores in the capable hands of their managers. She kept an eye on the operations to ensure they ran smoothly.

Inspired by my father's service, I decided that I wanted to enroll in military school. Though my family tried to talk me out of it, I was determined that I would be just like my dad. Arriving at the school, I inadvertently checked in with the upper-level students, and since I was a young man of large proportions, I was told that I could remain in that group. *Sure,* I figured. *Why not?* But I was two years younger than the others and not what you would call nimble on my feet.

Military schools were notorious for their hazing. If my room failed to pass muster or anything else was out of order, I would find myself sitting in a sink full of cold water. Or worse, I faced belt whippings and "saberings," in which I would be whacked with the side of a steel saber blade. I wrote a letter to my father in the Philippines about my predicament, and he wrote back.

My letter said, in essence: *Get me out of here!*

His reply: *I might try if you can do the same for me!*

I spent a year at that school, my entire eighth grade, and it was a nightmare.

Daddy returned home in 1946, and the family members began comparing notes about what the future should hold. The consensus was that the family should move to Nashville. The next generation was expanding. My little sister Doris was already a five-year-old, and we had three more little cousins. It was time to think more deeply about our heritage—and Nashville was a city with a larger Jewish community.

PULASKI'S JUDAICA LIBRARY

Many years after my boyhood in Pulaski, I often thought how I'd like to do something special for Martin College. I had offered donations through the years, but I wanted to do more.

Now, let me point out that Pulaski is a very Methodist town. Martin College has deep Methodist roots, and most of the students go into some form of church work—they become ministers and choir directors and missionaries. My family is Jewish, and many of those young people had never encountered a Jew.

"What if we started a Judaica program here?" I asked the college president, who applauded the idea. In memory of my parents, I had given a Judaica library to Vanderbilt University in Nashville, and we had enough duplicate books to provide Martin with a strong startup collection.

I figured we could get student rabbis to come down from Hebrew Union College in Cincinnati to give talks. The rabbi from a synagogue in Huntsville, Alabama, heard what we were doing and offered to teach a weekly class. Each year, we sent two or three students to Israel, and our only requirement was that each of them give three talks to civic groups. The program and speakers were popular not only among the collegians but among townspeople as well. That's the kind of effort that builds understanding between peoples of different faiths.

By then, the family was operating a chain of ten stores, with a Nashville warehouse to service them—but the Lewisburg cousin decided that he no longer wanted to be part of the chain. Splitting from the business, he took five stores with him. With only five stores to operate, my father and his partners no longer could justify the warehouse unless they pivoted their business model—and so, to remain profitable, they decided to head back into the wholesale business.

And that is how our family and our business were positioned in the postwar years on the cusp of the 1950s, the decade that would bring the baby boomers and the Cold War and the Civil Rights Movement. A long war had ended, and a new one was brewing. We were together, for now, in Nashville, and our family gatherings included a growing babble of little voices. We would be making our way now as wholesalers, not shopkeepers.

Our family would hold on to the remaining five stores until 1952. The buyer was Kuhn Brothers, a growing business that would expand in the ensuing decades into a chain of dozens of Big K stores before merging with Walmart in 1981. In our Pulaski days, we competed with a Kuhn's store on the square. Just a few years after my parents opened for business, that Kuhn's store tripled in size. It became the big store in town; we were the little one. Later, in Nashville, my parents got to better know the Kuhn family that had purchased our chain of five-and-tens. Their big store, they said, never could manage to outsell the little one in certain items, such as glassware and aluminum ware. I credit that to my father's insights. He knew his market and his customers, and he built up a loyalty to his store that continued long after our family left that town.

At the turn of the decade, I was a teenager of seventeen, still working with my parents but soon to head off to college and a stint in the Army. For now, my job in the family business was to service a new endeavor supplying merchandise for housewares racks in grocery stores. After school I would drive around Nashville, from store to store, delivering new items for the racks and picking up whatever hadn't been selling.

This wasn't my first experience in handling housewares. My father had long seemed to have an affinity for them. One of my jobs in Pulaski had been to unpack the dishes and tumblers he ordered, then sweep up the packing straw that fell from the crates and barrels onto the basement floor. Sweeping straw from a dirt floor is a slow, lonely, thankless task. By comparison, servicing the housewares racks was a joy. I was out and about and meeting people. I fancied myself an enterprising young businessman, and I wanted more of that feeling. We called this new endeavor "Service Wholesale." The name of a brand had begun to take shape.

It's the 1950s ...

- The Korean War drags to a stalemate as nuclear arsenals grow.

- The Salk vaccine promises to conquer polio.

- The Supreme Court declares racial segregation unconstitutional.

- The first color TV sets go on the market.

- The Soviets launch Sputnik, and the space race is on.

   ... and as the decade ends, Service Merchandise is born.

Through the Years ...

- 1950–54: Raymond attends college in Miami and Memphis.

- 1951: Family begins supporting Muscular Dystrophy Association.

- 1952: Service Wholesale subsidiary expands to Memphis.

- 1954: Company closes subsidiary but keeps Service Wholesale name.

- 1954–56: Raymond serves in the Army.

- 1956: Harry and Raymond Zimmerman become fifty-fifty partners.

- 1957: Service Wholesale contracts with *Romper Room* for toy sales.

- 1958–59: Hula-Hoops and Barbie Doll sales help to propel profits.

CHAPTER 2

Wholesale Growth, 1950–1960

A MILD AND RAINY Nashville morning in late January turned into an icy evening as the mercury plunged. For three days the Great Blizzard of '51 buried the region under eight inches of dense slush, snapping tree branches and power lines, collapsing roofs, and paralyzing a region unaccustomed to such winter fury. I was basking in Miami sunshine at the time, ostensibly studying, and I was in no hurry to go home from college to pick up a shovel. What happened that week, though, would become the stuff of legacy, influencing the lives of my family and many others over the years.

During the storm and for days afterward, our house was one of the few in Nashville that still had electric service and heat. My parents, being who they were, invited all their neighbors to take shelter in our home—including the Sandlers, whose son Billy had muscular dystrophy. During their stay, my parents got an up-close look at and deeper appreciation for what it takes to cope with that debilitating disease. After the storm, they immediately began working with Billy's mom, Ethel, to raise funds for the Muscular Dystrophy Association (MDA), founded just a year earlier.

Thus began our family's decades-long dedication to philanthropy. It became a family mission, with the MDA at the forefront. As our business grew locally and then nationally, we would expand the definition of family to include all those who worked with us. Starting in the 1960s, Service Merchandise would become a major participant in the Jerry Lewis MDA telethon, which raised $2.45 billion during the forty-four years that the entertainer hosted the Labor Day weekend event. We supported numerous other charitable causes as well—more on those efforts in the chapters ahead—but the genesis of the generosity was that 1951 ice storm. Out of hardship, so often, comes inspiration and progress.

A Detour through College

My parents were determined that I should go to college. I had been a happy teenager bouncing around Nashville, servicing the housewares racks in grocery stores for our Service Wholesale subsidiary. To please them, I managed to get a last-minute admission to the University of Miami. I figured I already knew a thing or two about business, having grown up in a family of merchants who were the children of merchants, but I was open to hearing what the academic types had to say.

I did enjoy some of my courses, mainly because the professors had done their time in the business world, and I respected their insights. My accounting professor was a retired General Motors comptroller, and my history professor had been the vice president of Studebaker.

They weren't merely teaching about accounting and history. They were teaching about life, and they brought it to life. They made it real.

Other classes, though, were simply unreal. One professor, on the first day of class, had us reading from a textbook he had authored, including a passage proclaiming that the sole purpose of business was to serve the community, not to make money. Really? Nothing wrong with service, of course—after all, "Service Wholesale" was the name of our housewares sideline. And ever since I was a little boy, my parents had drilled into me the importance of taking good care of the customer. But for this guy to suggest that making money didn't matter? That a business existed only for the good of the people? I imagined what Daddy would say: *What are you doing in that Communist school!* I had taken a seat next to the door, so I was able to quickly slip out of the lecture hall. I didn't return.

After two years in Miami, I was eager to get back to Tennessee and back to real life. During a trip home, I saw an opportunity to further expand our housewares sideline beyond Nashville. While visiting family in Memphis, my father and I stopped at a grocery and noticed that it was devoid of housewares. We asked if we might speak to the owner.

"Your shoppers come in here to buy food," I told him, "but they're also going to be looking to buy what it takes to prepare it." I explained how the housewares racks would work.

"Yessir. Makes sense to me," the store owner said. "And I bet it would make sense for a lot of other stores. You ought to sit down with the wholesale grocer who supplies us."

We did. The wholesaler escorted us to his office, listened to the pitch—and liked what he heard. It seemed a good way to move goods and make some money for all involved, while providing an added service for the customers.

"How many stores y'all thinking you need?" he asked my father.

I didn't wait for his response. "Fifty!" I blurted out, tapping the table decisively with a forefinger.

"We can handle fifty, sir, for sure." My father shifted in his chair but said nothing.

The wholesale grocer looked at me, then at my father, and nodded. He pulled a list of stores from his desk drawer and began checking them off.

Out in the car, Daddy turned to me and studied my face for a moment. "Fifty, Son?"

"Seemed about right," I said softly, my confidence ebbing. We both knew that I had a way of putting my mouth in gear before putting my mind in gear.

My father sighed. "And just who do you suppose will go around servicing all those stores? You?"

"Sure, I know I can do it," I said and then spilled out what had been weighing on my heart. "Miami's not for me, Daddy. I can transfer to Memphis State here and have plenty of time to keep those stores supplied."

He looked into my eyes and slowly smiled. He never seemed to stand in the way of what I wanted to do.

And so, after two years in Florida, I was back in my home state. I scheduled my college classes to maximize my time on the job, determined to do what I'd said I would do. We ran three trucks to those fifty grocery stores, and I had three helpers. Each morning, I checked the warehouse for inventory. After my classes I scheduled deliveries and pickups. I didn't study much. Instead, I spent my evenings going out with friends. I was nearly twenty, quite the man. I had a car, a job I liked, and a little money to spend. I was living the life.

I knew what was coming, though. My military duty was waiting. The understanding with my family was that I would stay in school and run the Memphis warehouse during my deferment. Meanwhile, my cousin—the son of my dad's partner—already was serving in the Army. Upon his discharge, I was to take my turn serving my country while he took a turn running the warehouse.

By 1954, however, it was clear that our housewares experiment wasn't going to be very profitable, either in Nashville or Memphis, so we shut the subsidiary down—but we kept the name. Service Wholesale would become the moniker for our entire operation.

In my last semester at Memphis State that year, I didn't even bother taking the finals. I had managed to get decent grades during my college career, even without much studying, but I ended that semester with straight Ds, and I didn't graduate.

As my college career was waning, I went out one evening with a drinking buddy, George. He had a job with a wholesale dry goods company. "This is goodbye, pal," he told me after we had lifted a beer or two. "I'm leaving too."

"Say it isn't so, George. What's up?"

"I'm going to work with my brother—he's a candy wholesaler. And he's got this great idea, Raymond. See, we figure we can send out a catalog, and folks will come to our store and shop from that catalog, or whatever." He was vague about the details.

I took a swallow and lowered my beer slowly. How could I put this delicately? "Well, George, let me just say you ought to stay on good terms with the dry goods place. You may need to go back there." He looked puzzled. "This catalog thing you're talking about … sounds to me like a really stupid idea."

No longer enrolled as a student at Memphis State, I soon got the "Uncle Sam wants you" letter. I'd known all along that this time would come, and I was ready. I left for basic training in December 1954. I knew, at least, that I wouldn't be going to Korea. The fighting there had ended.

Looking back on those days, I regret that I didn't pay more attention to my studies. You get out of college what you put into it, and I didn't put much in. To me, college was just getting in the way of getting on with life. It was a detour on my road to success. My parents insisted that I go, but what I really wanted to do was what they were doing.

> *Whatever you choose to do in this world ... you'll get out of it what you put into it.*

It wasn't until I had a few gray hairs that I understood what my college experience had done for me. I had begun to discover how much was out there. Whenever young people asked my advice, I emphasized the value of a liberal arts education. "You need to find out about the world, to get to know all sorts of different people, and to get to know yourself," I said. I told them that there's more to life than money, but that money matters because it helps us get more out of life. "Whatever you choose to do in this world," I said, "you'll get out of it what you put into it."

Armed and Ready

As the drill sergeant was ordering our squad out to the rifle range, he turned to a tall, scrawny kid in the lineup of recruits. "Johnson!" he said. "While we're out there, you'll be manning the telephone. Move!"

"The ... the *what*, Sergeant?" the young man stuttered. *Was he kidding?* I expected he would get slammed for such disrespect.

The sergeant scowled. "The telephone, soldier! You're manning the telephone. Go!"

"What's a telephone, Sergeant?" Johnson's eyes were blank. I could tell that he was serious. He didn't know. Johnson was a backwoods boy with little or no schooling who, if he ever had seen a telephone, had forgotten what the thing was called. He could neither read nor write.

Such was a scene from my basic training in Fort Knox, Kentucky. The year was 1954, and I was twenty-one years old. Johnson was not the only young man among us who had such challenges. In my Army days, I met many people whose lives had been nothing like mine. Some were smarter. Some were from wealthy families. Some were streetwise. Some were countryfolk. I learned to get along with them all and appreciate our differences. Like college, the Army broadened my experience with life, except that my college years were a time of freedom and exploration that expanded my mind. My Army years were a time of utter dependence and control—like a regression to childhood, in a way, for young men training to be warriors. The objective was not to expand the mind. The objective was to mold soldiers who would not blink at following orders, and that requires structure, efficiency, and unflinching discipline.

There were two hills at Fort Knox called Misery and Agony—and that pretty much says it all. My fellow recruits and I were compelled to run up and down them repeatedly, and I was inevitably the slowest, sometimes missing meal call as I plodded back to the mess hall. I felt as if I were twelve years old again and back in military school. As part of the basic training, we bivouacked in pup tents for three or four nights on the slopes of Agony, and I do not believe I ever have been colder in all my days. To set up our tents, we had to thaw the ground with a blowtorch so we could pound in the stakes.

Tough as they were, those eight weeks of basic training helped to shape my outlook. I believe that when this country did away with mandatory military service, we deprived young people of an opportunity to grow and gain new perspectives. I stood side by side with guys who didn't look like me or share my background or beliefs, yet together we were learning to deal with whatever we might encounter. Today it was the drill sergeant shouting in our faces. Tomorrow it could be the howl of a howitzer. We needed unity to face adversity. If we didn't pull together, if we didn't each do our part, we would never make it through. In that short time, I came to understand that the kids from Brooklyn or Chicago or San Francisco—or from Pulaski, Tennessee—were very much the same, brothers all.

I suppose that means I could have called Audie Murphy a brother, too, particularly since I was assigned, after basic training, to the Third Infantry Division based at the time at Fort Benning, Georgia. That was the same division in which Murphy served as one of the most decorated combat soldiers of World War II. My military career was somewhat less action packed. I became, by the luck of the draw, a clerk-typist. I sat in my office, without all that much to do, watching through the window as exhausted infantry soldiers trudged through the mud. On weekend furloughs, I regularly would leave base and travel a hundred miles to party with a college friend living in Atlanta.

And so the seasons of my service passed until, after two years, my duty was fulfilled. And what next? On the September day when I packed to leave, I went to see my company commander. "I'm thinking I'll go back to college," I told him—but not really. I only knew then that I was going home. Soon I would be getting on with the life that I had known. The Army hadn't squelched my ingenuity. I was back on the scene, and I meant business.

Onward as Partners

In 1956, newly back in civilian life, I approached my father with a proposition. His partner, our cousin, was willing to sell me his interest in Service Wholesale Company for a minimal price of $30,000. Daddy and I sat down to talk about it.

"Even if I come into the business as a fifty-fifty partner," I told him, "I understand that some fifties are bigger than others. This will always be your business, Daddy, and I'll do what you tell me to do."

He nodded.

"Just one thing, though," I continued. "I want you to make me a promise. When you give me a job to do, I want you to let me do it without looking over my shoulder and correcting me every step of the way. Let me make some mistakes so I can learn."

He nodded again, smiling softly. I knew at that moment that he was proud of me and of what I could become. Our agreement that day became a pillar in our relationship as business partners in the decades ahead. "How do you do it?" others in the industry would ask him from time to time. "How do you manage to work so well with your son?" They had tried to partner with their kids and found it next to impossible. He delighted in telling them about our agreement.

My father was true to his word. He didn't protect me from my mistakes. He let me stumble and get back up on steadier feet. We would talk things through afterward, but he never stood in my way. Daddy gave me the space to grow and learn—and that speaks volumes about the character and wisdom of the man.

The very day I came home from military duty, I was called to business duty. My father had sent one of our ten salesmen to Owensboro, Kentucky, to write a toy order. The phone rang about noon.

"Sam was supposed to meet me here at ten o'clock," said the caller, a kindly sounding woman. "Do you suppose he's all right?"

I assured her that we would look into the matter and certainly get her toy order. I knew, though, that Sam wasn't all right. He was a bit smitten with the bottle.

I jumped in the car and headed out to Owensboro, arriving about three hours later.

"I'm sorry to be so demanding," the lady told me after I introduced myself. "It's just that here we are, well into September already, and I've got to get the shelves stocked for Christmas."

We sat on her sofa and paged through our catalog, a foot thick, to find the items that she had in mind—three of this, a dozen of that—and I wrote her order.

On the way home, I noticed a sign at a crossroads pointing to "Central City, 30 miles" and turned to follow it. *This is such a long way to come for just one order*, I thought. *Let's see what else I can drum up.* Pulling into town, I saw Buddy's Hardware Store on the corner. I parked out front, entered the store through the squeaking screen door, and there I had the pleasure of meeting Buddy and Hazel Becker. I introduced myself.

"Do you have any of those Tiny Tears dolls?" Hazel asked before I could even open our wholesale catalog.

"No, not this time, sorry to say, but we do have Betsy Wetsy."

They ordered sixty on the spot—not a bad showing for this little side trip. As I was leaving, they suggested I drive to Cave City, where Hazel's father had a hardware store. I did. There I got another nice order. Both remained loyal customers, and friends, throughout our wholesale days.

In those years, I was on the road all the time, it seemed. I took over a territory that went to Clarksville, Tennessee, and Hopkinsville,

Kentucky, and up to Bowling Green in a given week. The next week I'd go to Sparta, Woodbury, Livingston, and Monterey. Every three weeks, I'd call on all these stores and write orders.

On one of those trips, to Livingston, Tennessee, I noticed a large truck backed up to a Dollar General store, where workers were loading up all the merchandise to haul it away. On the window was a Store Closing sign. *Unfortunate,* I thought, *but hardly an unusual sight.* I didn't think anything more of it until that evening, when my route took me to Monterey, Tennessee. There I saw another Dollar General store, and on the window was a *Grand Opening* sign. And wasn't that the same truck parked around back? Stopping to investigate, I stepped inside.

"Didn't I see you closing down a store over in Livingston this morning?" I asked the manager.

"Yessir, that's right. That was us," he answered. "This is all the same stuff that was over there. We brought it here for today's opening."

I was impressed. They had moved the contents of that store, counters and all, in a day. *Now that's an organized system,* I thought. Dollar General was a new kid on the block. The first one opened in Kentucky in 1955 and, within a few years, had developed into a chain of dozens in our region. As I write this, there are well over sixteen thousand Dollar General stores across the country. That kind of growth requires a highly streamlined operating system. I made a mental note of what I observed that day in Monterey. It would prove to be useful for our own operations in the years ahead.

Good Play at *Romper Room*

As our wholesale business grew, we began to transition into specializing in toys. In the years ahead, toys would remain my niche as a buyer for our inventory. Sometimes I drifted back to those days in Pulaski when I was a five-year-old earnestly demonstrating to my buddies the toys that my parents were selling—and, all these years later, here was Raymond Zimmerman still at it. The "toy man" they called me.

In 1957, while attending the New York Toy Fair, I took an interest in the potential that a children's television show called *Romper Room* could offer for our wholesale toy sales. The show, which had begun airing four years earlier, featured several adorable tykes and a teacher who would lead them in games and songs and offer simple moral lessons. The show was franchised to local stations, which each had its own hostess and featured local children. In each episode, an outsize bumblebee named Mr. Do Bee would teach good behavior, as in "Do *bee* a good listener" and "Don't *bee* a poor loser." The teacher would end each show by addressing the TV audience through her "magic mirror": "I see Timmy and Jill! And oh, there's Cindy and Joey!"

The show's logos were a bumblebee and a jack-in-the-box, and retailers soon found that kids were attracted to toys that sported those logos and that had been featured on the show. As we learned how successful *Romper Room* sponsorship had been in other markets, Service Wholesale obtained a contract to become the show's toy sponsor, which made us the exclusive wholesaler of toys with the *Romper Room* logos. We began wholesaling those toys to the major store chains, such as Woolworths, Grant, Kress, and Sears. We also bought commercials on the show to promote other toys.

Hula-Hoops and Barbie Dolls

Not long after we hooked up with *Romper Room*, Service Wholesale began making big profits with another toy that had people from coast to coast swinging their hips. The Hula-Hoop craze of the late 1950s was a second big reason that we did so much toy business. Wham-O introduced the plastic version in 1958 but did not initially secure a patent. Soon a lot of other providers, recognizing a winner, were improvising various ways to make them.

One day, as I was leaving for a family function in Memphis, a salesman stopped by my office with a Hula-Hoop in hand. "Let me show you something you don't want to miss," he said, bouncing it on his wrist. "Isn't this neat? Folks can't get enough of this. And it's not just the kids; it's all ages." He declined to demonstrate his hip action, however, simply reassuring me that everyone would be wanting one.

I knew this fellow well. In those days, we would see the same salespeople repeatedly, and we learned whom we could trust—and this one had long since proved himself. I thought of my dad's advice: "When you find a salesman you can trust and he tells you to buy something, you should do it. He's looking out for you." I put in a minimum order of twelve dozen hoops, then headed off to Memphis to join my family.

"You're crazy!" my father said, laughing, when I told him about the Hula-Hoop order. "Why would you buy something like that?" He shook his head, half chuckling, half sighing.

"Well, let's just see," I said. "I think we could be onto something here." Daddy soon would acknowledge that it was a good move. For about four months, it seemed that all we sold, in addition to the *Romper Room* toys, were Hula-Hoops. The salesman was right; people couldn't get enough of them. And neither could we. The order price kept dropping. We were selling them at last week's price and buying them for this week's price. I was on the phone for hours calling every garden hose manufacturer and anyone else who might be able to fill the demand.

On one of those days, I returned a call to a fellow who told me he was making Hula-Hoops and wasn't far from our office. "I'll be right over!" I said. I asked my office manager to come with me. He was a handy guy who could help me evaluate the caller's operations.

"Here's how I do it," the caller said after greeting us. He picked up a length of tubing that he had purchased and bent it roughly into a hoop, fastening the ends together with a peg. Then he worked his hands around the hoop to shape it into a better circle.

"Why not use something to shape it around, like a tire? That would speed things up a lot," my office manager suggested. Soon this supplier was producing Hula-Hoops by the truckload, and we were selling them as fast as he could make them. We must have sold fifty of those truckloads.

The next year's toy show featured a new doll by Mattel called Chatty Cathy, who spoke one of eleven phrases at random after you pulled a string on her upper back. Though the retail price of fourteen dollars seemed outrageous then, the salesman insisted that the doll would be a "hot item." I asked him to call in a minimum order for twenty-four to be shipped to us as soon as possible. When I met up later with my father, who also was attending the toy show, I proudly told him what I had purchased.

"Raymond, that's never going to sell," he said. "We need to cancel that right away." He was adamant, so I tracked down the salesman—but it was too late.

"The shipment," he said, "already is underway."

Chatty Cathy was coming our way, with plenty to say: "I love you! ... I hurt myself! ... Please take me with you!"

We soon found that this doll was another hot item. I quickly found buyers, including the Woolworths in Nashville, which bought half of them. The Woolworths manager soon called me, though, to report that the Walgreens next door was undercutting the $14 retail price, selling the dolls for $12.88.

It was a Friday afternoon. "Okay, let me get you a credit by Monday for the difference," I told the manager. "That way you can lower your price."

On Monday he called me again, but it wasn't to follow up on the credit. "I sold every one of those Chatty Cathies over the weekend for the full price," he told me. "Can you get me twenty-four more?"

The 1959 Toy Fair brought more good tidings. I intended to put in a sizable order for an eight-inch miniature doll that we had found to be popular, selling many dozens. The doll had retailed for a dollar. "Sorry, that's been discontinued," the salesman for Horsman Doll, whom I knew well, informed me.

Disappointed, I headed for the lunchroom, where I began chatting with a Mattel salesman who was another longtime acquaintance. He told me about a new doll, eleven inches tall, that would retail for three dollars, along with a bridal gown accessory that also would retail for three dollars.

In April 1960, the third floor of our Nashville warehouse was stacked from floor to ceiling with Barbie dolls.

The pattern was predictable.

"You need to buy this one," the salesman said. "She's going to be big. You'll be seeing her everywhere." I wasn't immediately impressed—this was a doll just slightly bigger than Horsman's miniature that would be selling for triple the price. But I was hearing from a salesman I knew well and trusted.

"Go ahead," I said. "Ship me the minimum order."

And, again, my father's reaction: "Cancel that, Raymond. It's too expensive. It won't sell."

Barbie, of course, did sell—and astoundingly well. So did her bridal gown, and that year Mattel came out with a variety of dresses for her. I put in orders for every one of them.

Early the next year, at the 1960 Toy Fair, I was met with standing applause from the Mattel entourage. "You're one lucky man!" I was told. "We're on a strict allocation for Barbie, so everyone's orders will be based on what they ordered last year. And in your market area, nobody else but you wanted her—so you're getting the entire allocation for Nashville."

The shipment came quickly. Mattel couldn't possibly keep all the dolls it was making in storage, so the company delivered them early, not expecting payment until year's end. And so, a few weeks after the toy show, in April 1960, the third floor of our Nashville warehouse was stacked from floor to ceiling with Barbie dolls.

Taking Flight

The 1950s were my coming-of-age years. I learned a lot about people, about business, and about life. I gained a deeper understanding of whom to trust, when to trust, and how to trust. My parents taught me by example the value of charity and community service. I got to know people from backgrounds far different than my own. I discovered how big this world really is.

As the decade began, I was a kid of seventeen, half-heartedly heading off to college but preferring instead to help in the family business. Ten years later, I was a man of twenty-seven and a full partner with my father in the leadership of Service Wholesale Company—and though our roots were in retail, the wholesale business was where my parents and I fully intended to remain.

All that soon would change, and it began on an early January day of the new decade, when we were introduced to a concept that would alter our lives and fortunes forever. We didn't think about it for six months, and then it was full speed ahead. We were about to head back into retail—specifically, the catalog showroom business. It was nothing that my family invented—we were far from early innovators—but we would take the concept to new heights. We eventually would evolve into the Service Merchandise Company, with stores across the country, and that is how I would meet the much larger family that I still love today.

All progress requires change, and it often feels uncomfortable. In fact, it can be downright scary at times, but one must face those fears and overcome them. I often recall an incident not long after coming home from the Army. Instead of returning to college, I used my GI Bill benefit to take flying lessons in Nashville. On my first solo flight without my instructor, I had a close encounter with fear, both on takeoff and landing.

During training, I had been accustomed to flying with my instructor, who was quite a large man. In my solo takeoff, however, I didn't compensate for the difference in weight and came terrifyingly close to flipping the little Cessna. Then, while trying to land, I ran into an intense updraft. It took me three attempts, and I was deeply shaken when I finally touched down.

As I taxied toward the hangar, I saw several people, including my instructor, coming out to check on me, having witnessed my rough landing. Instead of coasting to a stop, I did a big left turn, throttled down the runway, and soared back up to the sky. I executed my flight maneuvers flawlessly and came in for a perfect landing.

"What were you *thinking*?" the instructor asked me as I stepped from the plane.

"I figured I'd better go right back up," I explained, "because otherwise I might never fly again."

That was a principle that I had learned from my father and that would serve me well, time and time again, for all my days. Life brings rough takeoffs and landings to us all. We all make mistakes, but the bigger mistake is to cease trying. Fear has the power to paralyze— and if you quit, that's it. When my son had a car accident as he was learning to drive, I made sure he got right back behind the wheel that day to cruise around the block. When I encountered disappointments in business, I moved forward with confidence, rebuilding and reassessing, knowing that other opportunities would come. I knew I had what it would take to get it right. I never hesitated to get back on the runway.

At the dawn of the 1960s, my father and mother and I had much to learn about running a business that would become much larger than anything we had experienced. We understood, though, that our priority must be to take care of the many people who would be depending on us. We knew that setbacks would come our way and that we had what it would take to face them. We would get right back up and get the job done. For success in any endeavor, that is an essential.

It's the 1960s ...

- The Cuban Missile Crisis puts the world on the edge of nuclear war.

- The Peace Corps attracts thousands of young volunteers.

- President Kennedy and Martin Luther King Jr. are assassinated.

- The Civil Rights Act is signed into law.

- Neil Armstrong takes the first steps on the moon.

  ... and Service Merchandise expands regionally to five stores.

Through the Years ...

- 1960: Service Wholesale goes retail with catalog "sideline."

- 1960: The Nashville warehouse becomes the first Service Merchandise store.

- 1961: The first full year's sales more than double projections.

- 1962: Service Merchandise switches to a much larger catalog.

- 1965: The Nashville store's capacity triples with the purchase of an adjacent building.

- 1967–69: The company opens four stores and expands to Memphis and Chattanooga.

CHAPTER 3

Into the Catalog Business, 1960–1970

"WE ARE GOING into the catalog business," my father announced at the dinner table one July evening in 1960. "We will open a retail showroom in the warehouse." Mother and I looked at each other, then at him, and nodded. There was nothing to say but "Okay." We trusted his judgment. For years, since our Pulaski days, he had been the force behind the expansion of our family business. He had set the pace from day one.

The concept was far from new. For years, consumers had been growing accustomed to catalogs. A showroom gave them the opportunity to come in to see displays of the catalog merchandise, place an order on the spot, and take it home right away from the warehouse. Various companies developed the business model long before we did.

"This will just be a sideline," Daddy said. "I'm not saying we're getting out of wholesale, but we can move a lot of merchandise this way." I thought of all those Barbie dolls and accessories stacked on the third floor of our warehouse, and my father's idea began to make a whole lot of sense. He projected $300,000 a year in sales. If we profited $50,000, well, that would be a nice piece of change on top of our wholesale earnings. "We'll get going on this right away," he informed us.

The idea had been incubating for six months. Not long after New Year's, my parents and I attended the housewares trade show in Chicago and met a couple they had known in Memphis who owned a company that sold merchandise from a catalog. They escorted us around the trade show, introducing us to the vendors featured in the catalog and teaching us how the business worked. Every step we took with them that day was a step toward our future. Until my father's announcement at the dinner table, though, we didn't talk about changing course. We were still solidly in the wholesale business. And, as it turned out, we would be the last company of any significance to enter the catalog showroom industry.

But which catalog should we choose? There were many. We went with the one that the Memphis couple had shown us. We began purchasing the listed merchandise and stocking it in our warehouse, along with our existing wholesale inventory. Service Wholesale was now in the catalog showroom business.

Our First Catalog

Once we decided to enter the business, we had to move fast. The catalog was going to press the next month. We ambitiously ordered twenty thousand—and then we had to scramble to figure out how to distribute them. We had no names or addresses for a mailing list.

One way to collect names is to collect phone books, a rich resource of business addresses. We needed the names and the addresses of places where people were likely to congregate and see our catalog—doctors' offices, grocery stores, hospitals, and the like—and we needed them quickly, so I set out to get them.

The Nashville phone book wasn't enough. We wanted to distribute our catalog throughout the region. Every weekend, I would visit the towns around Nashville to gather phone books. In the evenings, we would pore through them for the most likely prospects.

One weekend I took my little sister Sue with me on a seventy-five-mile drive down to Pulaski on Highway 31. She was only fourteen years old and had never been to the town where our parents had been shopkeepers and where her older sister, Doris, had been born. We headed south from Nashville, stopping briefly in Franklin, Spring Hill, Columbia, and other communities along the way—including Pulaski.

"That's our old five-and-ten," I said as I drove down First Street. "And there's where we lived for the first several years." She squinted out the window, slowly nodding. "And there's the old jail where the sheriff let us play cops and robbers in the cells." A few turns later, I showed her the Civil War–era hospital where Doris had been born. Closed for at least fifteen years, it had fallen into disrepair.

"Doris was born *there*? I can't believe she was born in a place like that!" Sue said. I assured her that the hospital hadn't looked like that when Doris came into the world. Doris might have had some vague memories as a toddler in Pulaski, but not Sue, who was thirteen years younger than me and had known only Nashville. After so many years of being an only child—and an only grandchild, for that matter—I was blessed to have been given two delightful little sisters. They each had unique and dynamic personalities, overflowing with a love that enlightened our lives. I wish I could say that I was as good a big brother to them as they were sisters to me. Doris and Sue each worked briefly for our company during the 1960s before marrying and raising fine families.

"Let me show you some more of where I grew up," I told Sue. "Pulaski's a great town, and it really hasn't changed much." There in the public square, the courthouse stood stately in the late summer sunshine, surrounded by an assortment of storefronts, including the EB Smith grocery, which sold everything bulk in barrels, and the Reeves Drug Store. Before heading back to Nashville, I drove out Highway 64 and showed Sue a fine two-story house with a big yard, the last home on the east side of town. Daddy and Mother had built it for $4,000 once they were confident that their five-and-ten was doing well.

Sue perked up. "That's where you lived, Raymond?"

"Yep. And that smaller building next to it was Mother's chicken coop." It was elaborate, with electric lights and heat—in fact, a later owner would renovate it into a residence.

Only two months after my father's decision, we mailed out our first batch of catalogs in mid-September of 1960. It was a ninety-six-page "general merchandise" catalog, which later would lead at least one confused customer to visit our store and congratulate us on our new branch. "Beg pardon, ma'am," I told her, "but we only have this one store." She had presumed we were a branch of General Merchandise Company in Milwaukee.

In the end, we were able to distribute only about five thousand catalogs in that first mailing—but it was a start. Word soon would get around that we were making inroads into retail. And within a few months, we would be saying farewell forever to our wholesale years.

Focus on Family

In the spring of 1960, a friend who was one of our wholesale customers pulled me aside to tell me that his niece, Alice, was coming to town. "Ask her out, Raymond," he suggested. "I think she'll say yes, and you'll be happy when she does." Not one to miss an opportunity, I did as he suggested, and Alice and I went on a date. And another. And another. At the end of December, once it was clear to us that we would be making enough money to support ourselves and a family, we married.

It was a marriage that would last for twenty years, until we went our separate ways in 1980. We had two children: Freddy was born in July of 1963, and Robyn came along in October of 1966. They were teenagers when we divorced, and Alice remained dedicated to them and involved in their lives. She played a major role in them becoming the wonderful, caring, family-oriented adults that they are today.

I think back fondly on those years when Freddy and Robyn were young and on the weekend getaways that I regularly shared with each of them and their friends. We had a lakeside double-wide trailer in Pulaski, and Freddy often would invite three or four buddies to join us on weekends, fishing and cooking and enjoying life. We went on a variety of other outings. I shared special times with Robyn and her friends, too, and those are memories that have endured for decades.

When Freddy was about fourteen, he and his friends enjoyed earning a little money now and then by working at one of our stores. I would pick them up after they had spent a busy day juggling boxes to fill customer orders, and I was impressed by how they had memorized the stock numbers of the best-selling items. They were smart and industrious, and as I praised them, I couldn't help thinking, *These kids are going to be our competition someday!*

Freddy enrolled in the Wharton business school in Philadelphia and studied marketing, and we arranged for him to have a summer job with us. "Where are you going to put him?" my mother asked me. And I thought of my own early days in the business and all those hours I spent in the warehouse after school. I had done anything asked of me, and I knew Freddy would too. I even had cleaned the toilets. I can sincerely say that, as a manager, I never asked anyone to do something that I had not done myself.

"Well, I'm thinking he could start in the warehouse for a while," I told her. "He could handle freight, unload the trucks—"

"No, no, no!" she said. "He's too smart for that."

"Mother, that's how I started out—"

"Well, he's smarter than you!"

I could see the trace of a smile at the corners of her mouth, but she was adamant and overruled me. We put Freddy in a job where he could better develop his marketing skills. After he graduated from college, he moved to Chicago and was selling airplanes before returning to Nashville and focusing on money management and investments.

THE SMART ONE

Frankly, as I think back on it, I suppose Mother had good reason to proclaim Freddy the smart one. When he was eight years old, in the summer of '71, he and I flew to Boston, rented a car, and headed up Route 1 toward Maine to check out a summer camp for him. We drove past a shopping center having its grand opening.

"There's a great place for us to put a store!" Freddy said.

I smiled at him. We had only five stores at the time, and Boston wasn't in our line of sight. But years later, it was—and I sent our vice president of real estate to Boston to scout out a location for us there. He called me a few days later to report he'd found a great spot.

He began, "There's a Gilchrist department store up here that's going out of business—"

"Oh, is it in Saugus?" I interrupted.

"Yeah."

"And is it a V-shaped shopping center with a Sears in the other corner?"

"Uh ... that's right," he said. "How in the world do you know that?"

I wouldn't tell him. I didn't tell him for years, but finally I explained that Freddy had picked out that location long before he did. That store turned out to be a great spot for us and was our entrance into the Boston region.

Robyn was particularly eager to work for our company. She wanted to live in New York City after graduating from college, though, and went there looking for job prospects. Eventually we brought her in to work in our New York jewelry office and put her through management training. When the manager there went out on sick leave, the staff suggested to me that they put Robyn in charge.

"On one condition," I said. "If she's not doing the job you expect, you need to move her out." She did a spectacular job, though, in everyone's estimation.

After she married, she and her husband considered moving to Nashville. I even built her an office next to mine, delighted at the prospect that three generations would be building our company together. They chose to move elsewhere, though. But to this day, I still run into vendors who remember her tenure in New York: "How's Robyn? She was so great running the office there!"

In the years after their mother and I parted ways, I would move on to find love again, but I am forever grateful that my marriage to Alice produced our two marvelous children. The closing months of 1960 were a time of intense anticipation, and the focus was firmly on family—both the family life on which Alice and I were embarking and the larger family that would be the customers and associates of our new business enterprise.

AN HONEST DAY'S WORK

When Alice and I were engaged to marry, I promised her father that she could return to college whenever she wanted. A few years later, in 1963, she did. She was commuting to Emory College in Atlanta and took a few courses at Vanderbilt to get her degree in criminal justice.

Inspired by her initiative, I looked into resuming my classes at Memphis State, where I had dropped out a decade earlier. When the registrar finally found my records, the recommendation came back that I would need to start over.

"It has been a while," they said, "and, well, there's the matter of your grades."

So that was that.

One night at dinner, Alice had a question for me: "How has Nancy been doing at her job?" Nancy was one of our recent hires, on the job about a month.

"Funny you should ask," I said. "We were just talking about her today at the office—she's absolutely terrific."

"Great to hear that! Did you know she's out on parole?" Alice asked. She knew because she was working in the criminal justice system.

"Really? What did she do?" I asked. I don't recall whether Alice even told me. And that wasn't the point. What impressed me was the quality of Nancy's work.

I talked to our human resources staff. "Let's give a chance to more people like her," I said. "These are folks who are really motivated to make it. That's the kind of people we want to hire." And so we did, from time to time. We also hired a variety of others whom many other employers were likely to overlook. We hired people from the new wave of Russian immigrants in the 1970s, for example. My own grandparents had been Russian immigrants. They found opportunity in this land. It was only fitting that we could repay in kind. We hired people from a spectrum of ethnicities who needed jobs. We hired workers with physical and other challenges, including the visually impaired and those hard of hearing. Anyone eager to do an honest day's work for a decent day's pay could get a shot with us. Our company culture was inclusive, and we took pride in that.

Through the years, we provided aid via various charities and furnished apartments for people in need. At Christmastime, we held a toy drive at our corporate office. Those were just a few of the ways in which we strived to step up to the plate as good corporate citizens.

New Look, New Identity

Our first store was our warehouse at 305 Broadway, in the Nashville furniture district. Our showroom was nothing fancy. The place was vintage warehouse, with bare walls and wooden floors layered in linoleum. Lacking fixtures, we stacked much of the incoming merchandise on the floor in bulk. We did need to buy some jewelry cases since nearly half of the 1,200 or so items in our small catalog were jewelry. The rest went into stacks.

Our new venture soon caught the attention of the Federal Trade Commission (FTC). "Service *Wholesale?* This is retail," the FTC said, maintaining that the word "wholesale" in the company name could mislead consumers. Rather than risk a run-in with the regulators, we changed our name—and Service Merchandise was born.

Soon after our return to retail, complications set in. When our wholesale customers caught wind of our catalog mailing, most of them stopped trading with us. In their eyes, we were retail just like them and had become their competition. So why should they buy from us? It was a sobering situation. How could we make up in showroom sales what we stood to lose in wholesale? All those Barbies were depending on us to find them good homes.

To make matters worse, the *Romper Room* folks no longer wanted us as their distributors. When they found out that we were in retail, they lost confidence that we would be able to distribute their branded toys anymore to wholesale buyers. They didn't want their merchandise discounted directly to the consumer, so they made it clear that they would find a new distributor.

We still had our contract with the TV station through the remainder of the year, however. We used our time under that contract to have the *Romper Room* teacher hold up copies of our catalogs to show the broadcast audience the toys we had for sale, along with our variety of other merchandise. "Come to Service Merchandise for wholesale prices on these toys and much more!" Though we no longer carried the exclusive *Romper Room* toys, we still could direct the show's many viewers straight to us.

And it worked. From the start, Service Merchandise had a powerful TV connection. The show was so popular that five hundred letters a week arrived from kids too young to read or write. They got their mommies and daddies to help them. On the air, the teacher talked about more than the toys that we had for the little ones. She talked about the jewelry and housewares and gifts for Mom and Dad. The advertising on the show attracted a ton of attention to our store.

It was *Romper Room* and our stash of Barbie dolls that got us off the ground. We were on a reasonable pace that would keep us on track toward Daddy's estimate that we would have $300,000 in sales after a year. Then came December. We anticipated doing $75,000 in sales for the Christmas season. We did $172,000. The Barbies led the charge. Our generous supply of the dolls accounted for at least a quarter of those holiday sales, along with the toys that the *Romper Room* teacher was plugging for us.

Meanwhile, because our catalogs were going out to other cities in the region (Huntsville, Alabama, for example), we were getting merchandise orders through the mail too. I would pick them up daily at the post office and lay in bed till midnight, with a quart of chocolate milk and a package of Oreos, processing the orders. That was how I spent many November and December evenings for a few years. I would get to the store at 6:00 a.m. and prepare the shipments before the store opened at 9:00. There weren't many, perhaps a dozen a day, but it took hours to deal with them.

My father decided who would specialize in buying which merchandise. My job, as the obedient son, was to keep my mouth shut and my ears open. Daddy bought all the jewelry and the silver and left the silver-plated trays and such to me. He also loved buying the battery-operated transistor radios that were all the rage. I got to order the plug-in radios. "Here's what I want to buy," he would say, "and you take care of everything else." Though we were fifty-fifty partners, he was also the father—and with Mother on his side, it wasn't exactly an equal split. No matter. I respected the two of them deeply.

The Momentum Builds

Eager customers crowded into our showroom during that first holiday shopping season. "If someone were to faint out there," my father remarked to me on a bustling day in December 1961, "they wouldn't have room to fall down. There's standing room only!" Our eyes met. We both were thinking the same thing: *Wouldn't it be great if word got out that the fire marshal had to come here?*

We made sure that happened and placed an anonymous call. "Too many people in here!" the fire marshal admonished us after working his way through the throng to find us in the office. "You can't do this."

"Yessir," my father told him. "What do you suggest?"

The fire marshal advised us to post somebody at the door to stop people from entering until others had left, and we dutifully did as he said. We also called the radio station and the newspaper with a tip about some big fuss going on at the store, where a long line quickly formed outside.

With every problem comes an opportunity.

Later, on the evening news, we heard this report: "The Service Merchandise store at Third and Broadway had to work with city officials today to regulate a crowd of holiday shoppers eager to enter." The reporter then interviewed a customer.

"You bet we're excited!" she said. "We've never seen prices like this!"

With every problem comes an opportunity. The fire marshal was correct; we had allowed too many people into our store, and we couldn't do that. But here's something we proved that we could do: we brought in $30,000 in sales just in that one day. It was another milestone for us—and the momentum was building.

Our catalog "sideline" continued to make a lot more money than we had anticipated. The figures, which were strong and getting stronger, allowed for only one conclusion. It was time to get out of wholesale altogether and devote everything to this new endeavor. By January, we had moved full-time into the catalog showroom business. We set about liquidating our wholesale inventory to free up space and money. By May of 1961, we had sold all our leftover wholesale inventory.

Soon we were reassessing the $300,000 that my father had projected for the first year's sales. We closed out 1961 with $700,000 in sales—and the next year we did a million. We had found a business model that clearly would be central to our growth and our identity. In a decade, as we expanded regionally, we would surpass $40 million in sales. A decade later, expanding nationally, we would hit a billion, on our way to $4 billion by the mid-1990s. In the chapters ahead, we will track our growth to 406 stores in thirty-seven states. We were building more than a business. We were building a devoted family of associates who still fondly recall their years of service, from the stockrooms to the boardrooms.

VISITS FROM THE STARS

Our original store in Nashville wasn't far from the Grand Ole Opry, and a number of high-profile stars came in to shop with us. To name a few: Larry Gatlin, the Judds, June Carter, Mother Maybelle, Johnny Cash—and, yes, Elvis. Elvis had been to our Memphis store and in Nashville, too, when he was in town recording.

I recall one visit by a well-known star who seemed captivated by a $320 watch on display at our jewelry counter. He seemed a bit unsteady on his feet. In my opinion, it was the ugliest watch we had, but this gentleman (who shall remain unidentified) peered at it as if it were his heart's desire. "I'll buy it," he said. He fumbled for his wallet and pulled out three hundred-dollar bills.

"Sorry, 's'all I got," he said.

"Sold!" I said. I was eager to get this watch out of our inventory.

Early Initiatives

It's one thing to find a business model to propel growth; it's quite another to know how to handle that growth. By early 1962, we realized that we needed help learning to run a larger store. For years we had been doers. We needed to become delegators. To get started, we hired the manager of a local discount store to manage our store. It was clear we were onto a good thing. We knew we could expand but didn't know how or where or when.

In the slow months after the holiday season, we began looking for systems to improve operations. Our first attempt at automating our point-of-sales was the Kimball system, which used perforated sticker tags that we attached to the merchandise. At checkout, the cashiers would rip off half the tag, and at day's end the tags would be fed into a machine to generate inventory reports. It should have been efficient, but it didn't work for us. The stickers didn't hold for long, and the tags would peel off the merchandise. Not only did that make a mess of the floor, but the missing tags meant that the reports would be missing data. We had no choice but to track the inventory manually. The Kimball system was a disaster.

We also tried, for a while, having the customers write down the price of the item from the catalog—but that didn't work out either. They would put down the wrong numbers sometimes, or the writing would be illegible, and it would take far too long to verify the price. We used one machine to keypunch what the customer had written and another machine to verify the accuracy. The process was so cumbersome that we feared it was slowing sales.

As we transitioned out of the wholesale business, we experimented for a few years with a membership card system. It was the sort of system that a few warehouse stores, such as Sam's Club, Costco, and BJ's Wholesale Club, still use today. Back then, membership cards were a common means of building mailing lists. Our card was free and easy to obtain. To qualify, you had to be a government employee, an employee of a business, or pretty much anything. Actually, we would joke that you had to be alive or dead to qualify for a card. The card was our attempt to bridge the worlds of wholesale and retail, but we soon left the wholesale part of our business behind. We had become direct to consumer, and the card really served no purpose.

One day, as my father and I were assisting a shopper with a purchase, she remarked that she had forgotten her membership card on an earlier visit and had ended up going to a competitor instead. Daddy kept his cool, so far as anyone but me could see. I could tell he was simmering inside. He offered his regrets to the shopper, finished helping her with her selection, and motioned for me to join him in the office. I closed the door, and he turned to me. "Get rid of the damned cards," he said. And that settled the matter. He had no patience with anything that could inconvenience the customer and get in the way of sales.

An Evolution in Catalogs

At the time we entered the industry, the advertising power of catalogs was potent. They propelled demand and sales. If the hottest item in this year's catalog wasn't included in next year's catalog, it would cease selling. In the fall of 1960 and throughout the next year, we tried to stock everything listed in our catalog. We didn't want customers coming in just to hear our regrets that we didn't have what they wanted but could order it.

One day, a fellow merchant in town paid us a visit. Nashville wasn't all that big, and we stayed on friendly terms with other businesses, who often offered good advice. He noticed that we had received a shipment of water skis for our spring catalog. "You'll go broke if you try to stock everything," he said. "If somebody wants an item, just have the manufacturer drop-ship it to you directly."

Catalogs had improved markedly by this time. Initially, the pages were grouped by manufacturer, not by the type of product sold. The vendor would submit its page for a catalog with the intention of focusing attention on a few of its top products. Then, to fill the rest of the space, the vendor would throw in fifteen or twenty other items. Those were much less likely to sell even if stores stocked them, which they didn't.

Norelco, for example, was eager to feature its new electric razor. To warrant a catalog page, the company needed to complete a full page, front and back—but it only wanted to peddle the one item. So it had to include an assortment of accessories that customers weren't interested in purchasing through the catalog.

It was time for a more sensible and customer-friendly approach. The catalogs began putting similar products from multiple manufacturers together on the same pages so consumers could easily find what they wanted. Essentially, the catalogers said to the manufacturers: *Look, you're paying a bundle to produce these pages, so why don't you give that money to us instead, and we'll choose the items and make our own pages.*

Soon, catalog groups were featuring the merchandise from several vendors on a single page—merchandise that made sense for the stores to keep in stock for the customers. Gone were the extraneous page fillers that cluttered the catalog. Every page had multiple items that potentially would sell well.

By January 1962, impressed by our success and facing the prospect of increasing competition coming to town, we wanted a bigger catalog. We chose one with four hundred pages printed by Creative Merchandising, a division of Modern Merchandising. With that catalog, we found our footing and our business took off, setting the stage for our expansion and, eventually, our decision to go public.

Into Memphis and Chattanooga

By 1965, Service Merchandise was doing so well that we bought the building next door to us, which was twice the size of the original warehouse, and substantially increased our capacity. At that point, we were doing about $3 million a year in revenue. That put us in a position where we potentially could expand to other locations.

Frankly, we were leery of ever having more than our one store in Nashville. We had observed, even back in the wholesale business, that a lot of companies failed when they opened a second store. In fact, the highest percentage of failures come then, not later with multiple stores. Why? Because there's a lot more to do, and often the business lacks both a management team and sufficient financing. Any time we saw companies opening a second store, we would have our doubts about how successful they would be.

Two years later, however, we heard from the couple who back in 1960 had introduced us to the catalog business at the Chicago house-wares fair. Would we be interested in purchasing their company, Celmax? There was a nice circularity to that deal. Without their influence, we might never have entered the industry. That couple brought us into it, and now they wanted us to be their buyers as they headed out of it. Our purchase of their store put Service Merchandise into the Memphis market. The Nashville operation was now the flagship.

Meanwhile, even before the purchase went through, we had been looking to open another store. We put out the word that we were in the market to expand. We got a call one day from a store in Madison, a suburb of Nashville. Daddy liked its dimensions. It was small, only one hundred feet by seventy-five feet, but the hundred feet was its width—all the better to put as much merchandise as possible up near the registers. We visited the store within an hour after that call and bought it. That became our third store, and it opened just days after we opened in Memphis.

If there was anything to our concern about businesses failing with a second location, I can say that we never had only two stores. We jumped from one to three. And we soon added another store in Memphis. Both Memphis stores were small compared with our flagship, but they generated plenty of sales.

In 1969, we entered the Chattanooga market, about 130 miles southeast of Nashville. We leased a small store there that we soon moved to a larger location up the street, although we kept both open during the Christmas rush that year. That put our total store count at five as the decade ended.

Ready for the Next Level

Those were hectic years. I found myself hustling around the clock, it seemed, to keep up. When we had just one store, Daddy and I split the responsibility for buying inventory, but it was my job alone to pay all the bills. That pattern continued as we added more stores, which meant a lot more buying and a lot more bill paying.

As our business grew, I was keenly aware that our inventory expenses were growing too. Concerned about the cash flow, I tended to purchase too little. It wasn't that we couldn't have sold more—our sales records certainly justified greater quantities—but I was finding it hard to add the extra zeros. As a result, my share of the inventory was often low or out of stock.

"Raymond, you need to start buying more," Daddy finally told me. "If people come in here and can't get what they want, they'll get it somewhere else—and they might never come through our doors again. So either you need to buy more or we'll have to get somebody to do it, someone who will get the job done." In our family, it was far worse to buy too little and lose a sale forever than to buy too much and wait to sell it.

"Get somebody then," I said. "There's plenty else I can be doing." After that, I began spending more time on the financial end, until we grew to the point where we had a larger staff and brought in a chief financial officer. I eventually focused most of my time on the IT and real estate sides of our business.

A major challenge of those early growing years was to make sure that our merchandise was counted and cataloged and that every store had sufficient inventory to meet demand. At six in the morning, I would arrive at our flagship store, and I visited each of the others at least once a week. Late at night, I still would be writing orders.

We had yet to develop an automated inventory system that functioned well. Doing it manually was laborious, but my father had drilled into me the importance of accounting for inventory before purchasing. That might seem elementary, but when you introduce human error to the equation, anything can happen.

Case in point: The Madison store manager called me one day to ask that at least six more pieces of lawn furniture be delivered there as soon as possible. *Six?* I couldn't imagine that tiny store would need so many.

"Could you double-check your inventory first?" I asked.

"Sure, but I saw it with my own eyes," he said. "We've already sold twelve." He had an elevated office with a view of the sales floor. "They're going like hotcakes."

A few minutes later, he came back on the phone, perplexed. He still had several in the inventory and had sold only a couple. It turned out that some of the buyers hadn't been able to fit the furniture in their cars and brought it back in. The manager had been seeing the same merchandise passing back and forth.

Overall, though, we were sending plenty of merchandise out the doors of our stores and into the homes of customers, who were growing loyal to our brand. Small businesses often get in trouble as they expand, but we had a strategy of simplicity and innovation at every step to keep ahead of the competition. We were open to learning, day by day, better ways to run our operation. By the start of the 1970s, we were ready for the next level. Thanks to the hard work of our associates, Service Merchandise in a few years would go public and expand into a nationwide enterprise.

Our Competitive Edge

I close my eyes, and I still can see Mother behind the jewelry counter in those early days, smiling radiantly as she talked to customers. She was the ultimate saleslady, with a style and grace so attractive that people would come in asking for only her to serve them. And there was nothing superficial about her charm. She told the truth, straight up. You always knew where you stood with her. For as long as she lived, she was integral to our company. She knew our products well, and she dealt with people squarely. Our customers appreciated that.

In this memoir, I could never come close to naming all the many thousands who were of tremendous service to Service Merchandise through the years. Were I to name any, I'd worry that I was neglecting many—and each and all possessed qualities that drove our success. I can single out my mother here because, well, she was my mother. But so many others had the character and charisma that kept our customers coming back, and to each I am eternally grateful.

From the first employee we hired outside our family to the one who turned out the lights for the last time, we built a great company together. I paid visits to all our stores and can still see, in my mind's eye, the bright faces of the salespeople and the cashiers as they greet the customers. I can see the warehouse workers, hustling to fill orders, and the many other backroom associates without whom we could not have sold a single thing. I recall our buyers who selected our diamonds and toys and gifts, who spotted

It was our people, our Service Merchandise family, who were central to our success.

consumer trends so we could deliver just what the people wanted. And, of course, the wide variety of vendors who supplied the merchandise. All those folks, working together, worked magic. They were team players who collaborated with camaraderie. Each is part of the Service Merchandise legacy.

Sure, we had other things going for us, right from the start. We could price our merchandise less expensively because we still were listed as wholesalers and could buy direct from manufacturers.

Shoppers essentially could get from us the same price for an item that most stores would pay a distributor before marking it up. As our own wholesaler, we could buy large lots of merchandise such as jewelry, electronics, luggage, and other high-end goods.

And that's all well and good—yet it was our people, our Service Merchandise family, who were central to our success. It was they who truly gave us our competitive edge. I think again of my mother's smile and the kindness in her face as she dealt with our customers. She represents the countless people who were dedicated to delivering the best of service and merchandise.

It's the 1970s ...

- The Watergate scandal ends the Nixon presidency.

- Walt Disney World opens in Orlando, Florida.

- Home computers and video games make a commercial debut.

- With two oil crises, gas prices rise during the decade from thirty-six to eighty-six cents.

- The UPC barcode is introduced.

- Israel and Egypt sign Camp David peace accords.

- The US establishes diplomatic relations with China.

  ... and Service Merchandise rises to retail prominence nationwide.

Through the Years ...

- 1971: Service Merchandise goes public.

- 1971: A "clipboard" system is introduced to stores.

- 1972: The company opens its first store outside Tennessee.

- 1972–79: Stores open in multiple markets nationwide.

- 1973: Raymond Zimmerman becomes company president.

- 1979: At decade's end, there are 101 stores coast to coast.

- 1980: Service Merchandise publishes its own catalog.

CHAPTER 4

Coast to Coast, 1970–1980

SOMEWHERE, DEEP IN A BOX among mementoes of the past, is a photograph of me with my hair to my shoulders and a long, scraggly beard. It was the summer of '72, and looking at that picture you would think I was a hippie from Woodstock—but that wasn't my way at all. Instead, my ragged looks were the result of my habit, once again, of putting my mouth in gear before my mind could catch up. I had vowed not to shave or get a haircut until the stock price of Service Merchandise hit fifty dollars a share.

How did all this come about? Let's back up a year and find out—because something else was growing even faster than my hair. That something was our company, which was embarking on a decade of rapid expansion that would take us coast to coast. We began the 1970s with five stores, all in Tennessee, and $20 million in sales. We ended the decade with more than a hundred stores nationwide and $730 million in sales. The 1970s was the decade that our company grew to prominence as a major retail player and pacesetter in the catalog showroom industry.

In early 1971, my father and I didn't have any interest in transforming Service Merchandise into a publicly traded company. We already had what we felt was a large business to manage. The prospect of an initial public offering (IPO) wasn't on our radar, though we were aware that businesses similar to ours had gone public. We also had noted that Best Products, a major catalog retailer based in Richmond, Virginia, recently had begun trading on the New York Stock Exchange and that Modern Merchandising, another big player based in Minnesota, had begun trading in the OTC market. We were in the same catalog group as both.

Then an article appeared in *Barron's* suggesting that Service Merchandise was ripe for an IPO. The article included us as among companies that could be good prospects to go public.

As you can imagine, we soon were besieged by bankers eager for the lucrative opportunity of handling our IPO. Among them was the investment banking firm of Wheat & Company, which had taken Best Products public. I explained that we weren't really interested.

"Listen. Tell me which you'd rather own," the banker asked Daddy and me. "Would you rather own 100 percent of Service Merchandise as it is now or 3 percent of Sears Roebuck?" Okay, I saw his point. "So think of it this way," he continued. "After going public, you'll still own 80 percent of Service Merchandise, and you'll also have all this money. You can use it to grow on."

I looked at Daddy. "I think we should go public," I said.

"Okay," he said. "Let's do what you want to do."

At the time of that conversation, Wheat estimated that our company was worth $4 a share. The market was booming in those first few years of the 1970s, however. On the day of our IPO in November 1971, our stock opened at $14 at 9:00 a.m.—and it closed at 4:00 p.m. at $21.50.

We were ecstatic. A lot changed for Service Merchandise and for my family that day. Now that we were a public enterprise, we would be able to pursue things that had been out of our reach before. And we knew, too, that we weren't just looking out for ourselves anymore. We had to operate in a way that also would be best for our shareholders, employees, and customers. It was like starting a family. You become acutely aware of how much others are depending on you.

By January of 1972, the stock had hit $33 a share, and there was a rumor on Wall Street that we would be posting earnings of a dollar a share. No way. I knew that was too high. We had yet to do anything with the money from the IPO. The Street was now anticipating a dollar, though, and we didn't want to disappoint the investors when we issued our first earnings report. We needed to squelch that rumor right away—but regulations prohibited making any kind of announcement until ninety days after closing a deal.

We turned to our bankers at Wheat for a solution, and they approached the Securities and Exchange Commission (SEC) with a special request that we be allowed to announce that the rumor was unfounded. And the SEC, impressed that here was a company trying to lower expectations, not hype them up, not only allowed a press release but helped us to word it. We figured our stock would take a hit—and it did, for a couple of hours. It fell two dollars a share, then climbed right back up to $33.

I got to thinking about just what that meant. "Do you suppose," I asked Daddy, "that if people like our stock so much that it's at $33, maybe they'd like a little more?" We had yet to sell any of our personal stock holdings from the IPO, but we'd gotten a taste of the possibilities.

"We want to do a second offering," we told the folks at Wheat. "What do you think?" Sure, we could do that, they told us, but they estimated that we would lose 20 percent of the value of that stock—in other words, it would come in at about $26 a share.

Daddy and I talked it over. "You know, just a few months ago, we were figuring on coming in at $4," I pointed out. "So, really, is this a loss, or would it still be a big gain?" It was a gutsy thing to do. We hadn't spent a dime from our first stock offering, and now, almost right away, we would be asking for more. "People might think we're crazy," I said. My father and I locked eyes, and we smiled. "Let's do it," I said. He nodded.

Our strategy required careful timing. We planned the second offering to happen five months and twenty-seven days after the IPO. The tax structure of the time made all the difference. If you held an investment for six months or longer, you would be taxed at the favorable capital gains rate of 20 percent. But if you sold before six months, you would be taxed at the whopping 70 percent rate of ordinary income tax. A lot of our early investors had bought in at $14 and were looking at an attractive gain of nearly $20 a share. We wanted to beat that six-month threshold so that they would still be sitting tight waiting for the lower rate. We didn't want them selling and knocking down the price just as we were trying to cash in.

The timing didn't work out as we hoped. I got a last-minute call from our market maker: an OTC regulation was delaying the date that we could come out with our second offer, and it now would be six months and two days after the initial deal. So much for our strategy—the investors no longer would have the tax incentive to hang on to our stock a little longer.

I was livid. Nonetheless, we took a gamble and decided to go through with the second offer—and, instead of dropping, the stock price went up. We had worried that it would tumble down from $33 a share. Instead, it priced at $39.50 on the day of the deal. We hadn't lost 20 percent of the value of our shares, and the investors weren't rushing to cash in just to save on taxes. They were staying put. They recognized a good thing.

The market, once again, had beat our expectations. The nation was enjoying a boom year in 1972 on the eve of a two-year recession that would test the mettle of the industry—and it emerged just fine. It endured the inflationary years of that decade and a spike in gold prices that challenged jewelry sales. This was survival of the fittest, and the fittest grew strong. By all appearances, catalog showroom sales were here to stay. The consumers had spoken.

And that brings us back to my shaggy looks during that time. When I traveled to Richmond in November of 1971 to finalize that deal at Wheat & Company, I made a vow that I would come to regret.

"Raymond, you ought to let your hair and beard grow like so many other young guys these days," one of the bankers told me. "Just think of all the money you could save on razors!" It was all in fun, of course, but I decided to take it seriously.

"All right," I said. "I won't shave or get a haircut until our stock hits fifty dollars a share!" And I was true to my word. I grew steadily more hairy as our stock price grew steadily stronger. I didn't want to jinx a good thing, so I kept my distance from clippers. And then one midsummer day, shortly after the Fourth of July, our stock hit the magic number, and, after eight long months, my long locks were gone for good.

Looking back, I don't know why we felt ready to become a publicly traded company, any more than we were ready to go to the moon. At the time, we were only doing $18 million in sales in our five stores—two each in Nashville and Memphis, and one in Chattanooga—and even though we would nearly triple our number of stores that year, we didn't have the depth of management to run an organization of that size.

It all worked out somehow. Some of it was luck, sure, but as we grew, we learned—and we were blessed to have the help of remarkable people who helped us live up to our aspirations. Our rapid expansion couldn't be left to luck. We had a lot to discover about operating a company of such size, and we had the opportunity along the way to learn from some of the biggest figures in our industry. I met people in those days who would become like an extended family.

The years ahead would be a hectic and stressful time, but I was in my prime and eager for the challenge. And I found it gratifying to see my parents experiencing such success. They had come a long way from the Pulaski five-and-ten. They already had done what I still was waiting to do; they had proven themselves to the world. And now, as they continued to pursue even greater accomplishments, the excitement and enthusiasm made all the hard work feel like play.

Doing things right, in large part, means treating people right—and that would become deeply ingrained in our company culture.

About a year after we went public, I took on the role of company president and Daddy became chairman. The change of titles was just a formality, really. All of us knew that Daddy was still in charge—but being in charge doesn't mean you insist on calling all the shots. He generally wanted me to do as I wished. And what I wished, above all, was to do right by him and Mother. I appreciated that they trusted me with increasing responsibility. They always had, even after I messed up. Sometimes I thought back to that day when, as a little boy, I tried to pilfer that dime from the tray behind the counter. Even after that, my parents still trusted me to work the register. Through it all, they believed in me, and knowing how they felt made me all the more determined to do things right.

Doing things right, in large part, means treating people right—and that would become deeply ingrained in our company culture as we grew. An organization's spirit reflects the expectations and attitudes of the leadership. We would do well not just because our stores sold good merchandise at a better price but because we cultivated loyalty among our associates and gave them incentives to give us their best.

Full Speed Ahead

Our growth trajectory had begun. Within a few years, our company would be joining Best Products and Modern Merchandising as one of the "Big Three" in the industry, and we would continue to forge close business and personal relationships with them. The promise of the new influx of funding stoked our ambitions. By the end of the decade, we had risen to the top of the catalog store triumvirate.

Early on, we concluded that Service Merchandise needed to expand into some of the larger metropolitan areas of the Northeast, Midwest, and Southeast. We saw a pattern: our stores tended to have plenty of $100,000 days between Thanksgiving and Christmas, but afterward our sales dropped sharply, with a few spikes such as for Valentine's Day and Mother's Day. When we compared our sales to the sales of stores in our industry with similar revenues that operated in larger metropolitan areas, we observed that those stores never had a $100,000 day—but they didn't have a postholiday drop either. They kept a steadier pace through the year.

What was going on? No great mystery. Our customers tended to do more shopping in gift-giving seasons. The shoppers in the larger metro areas, who tended to have more discretionary income, spread their purchases throughout the year. So we resolved to add locations with that kind of demographic and build our sales volume with less volatility. We had the will—and finally, with the money from our back-to-back stock offerings, we had the way.

We located two sites, initially. We found real estate in Atlanta and then in Cincinnati and announced that we would build stores on those sites from the ground up. Our horizons then began expanding—*Why stop there? Let's do some more!*

We learned of a store that was available in Indianapolis, so we decided to be big shots and chartered a plane. On the way there, we stopped to see another site in Bloomington, Indiana. "Okay. We like this. We'll take it," we said as we walked through the store. Then it was onward to Indianapolis to consummate the deal there. The building was twice as big as we needed, but, hey, the rent was cheap. Two leases in one day.

We also had a friend in Indianapolis who owned a little store downtown called Warco Supply that used the same catalog that we used. He was ready to retire, but we didn't want to just roll into town and knock him out of the box. So we asked if we could buy his business. "Deal!" he said, and we worked out the price. We didn't particularly want that store, but it was the right thing to do.

Next, Oklahoma. We learned of two stores available in Oklahoma City, so I struck a deal with the owners to move into that market. Then, one morning, I read about a site in Tulsa; the Gibson discount chain was closing.

"Ever been to Tulsa?" I asked Daddy. "No? Well, I've booked a three o'clock flight for you and Mother."

Daddy called from Tulsa that evening. "Get on the next flight out here, Son. You've got to see this place. It's fabulous." So the next day, I landed in Tulsa, too, and within an hour the three of us were flying back home, the deal sealed.

It felt that even if a prospect fell through, it could lead to other opportunities. One of the places we wanted to go was Charlotte, North Carolina. We found an attractive lot there that was part of a shopping center. The shopping center's owner told me we could build on the lot only if we got the blessing of the Zayre discount store that was one of his longtime tenants. Zayre didn't want us competing there, but a store representative did give me a great tip about two sites the chain was closing in Columbus, Ohio.

"Tell me more," I said, and what he described sounded perfect for us. Columbus was a market that we were eager to enter. "We'll take them," I said, the sites unseen. I didn't put pen to paper, but I felt my word was my commitment. Still, I wanted my parents to give their blessing to the decision.

First we drove to the West Columbus location, and as we approached it, my father was impressed by how many new homes were under construction nearby. Had we driven any farther, he surely would have had second thoughts. The site was on the edge of town, with a hundred miles of nothing beyond. Then we headed toward the other store. The demographics there, according to my research, were great. What we were seeing out the window, however, was not so great. The neighborhood looked shabby and run down.

"No way are we opening here," Daddy said.

"This is dreadful," Mother chimed in. And I began to sweat. I'd given my word that we would take both locations. I made a few turns and cruised down the boulevard, and soon we were in the lovely, tree-lined suburb of Bexley, filled with magnificent homes—just a few blocks from the store.

"This will do," my father said, nodding as he looked around. "Let's sign for this one, too, Son." I allowed as to how that would no doubt be the right thing to do.

Service Merchandise was entering market after market. We weren't just Tennessee anymore. We now were Indiana, Ohio, and Oklahoma, and soon we picked up another site in Huntsville, Alabama. Back at the close of 1971, when we still had only our five Tennessee stores, the biggest had about twenty-five thousand square feet of sales space. At the close of 1972, we had fourteen stores, most of them sixty thousand square feet or larger, and we had more than doubled our annual sales to $40 million.

We opened another eight in '73 and eight more in '74, with no intention of slowing down. In fact, our pace quickened. In 1978 alone, we opened thirty-three locations, including twenty-two showrooms we acquired from Value House that gave us a foothold in several New England markets. That year we also acquired the B.A. Pargh Company, which at the time was a little office-supply firm with sales of about $300,000 a year. It continued to operate as a separate entity, and, ten or twelve years later, the managers had built it into a $50 million business—and they also were running our mail order division, which was another $50 million operation.

As we searched for places to plant stores, my parents and I at first looked primarily for communities that were relatively affluent so that we could bring in strong and steady sales without being so reliant on the holiday cycles. We were focusing on larger stores in metropolitan areas. By mid-decade, as we explored opportunities in smaller markets as well, we introduced a smaller store size appropriate for those communities.

My parents differed on their criteria for choosing locations. Daddy wanted to open stores near where a lot of new housing was being constructed. When he toured potential sites, he observed how many yards had swing sets and swimming pools, evidence of young families. Those families would be doing a lot of shopping, he figured, and would need a lot of the goods that our stores would stock. Mother, on the other hand, favored older neighborhoods with a lot of retirees. Those folks would have plenty of discretionary income now that their kids had left home, she reasoned. Both approaches made sense. So why choose? We did both. We weren't turning any good locations down.

Meanwhile, we never forgot our roots. Back in Nashville, we had five stores at one point, but we met customer after customer whose loyalties remained with our flagship. They favored that old warehouse over our other stores. Their feet just felt better walking that floor, they told us. They came for the charm, they said. We had prettier locations, modern and spacious. Anyone could see that. But charm? That's not something you see with your eyes. You see that with your heart.

The Clipboard Advantage

In 1971, even before we began acquiring all those stores, we made a major change that also would capture the hearts of our customers. Service Merchandise had adopted the "clipboard" system that became part and parcel to our identity. And we encouraged our associates to refer to our locations only as "showrooms," not as stores. That, too, was crucial in distinguishing ourselves from the competition.

Until that year, we had a rather standard checkout process. Customers would shop for merchandise stacked out on the sales floor and take their selections to the cashier to check out, the same as in any store. We had to ticket every item with its price, and those tags had to change whenever the price did. That was a labor expense that took time and money, and employees occasionally made mistakes while retagging. The price stickers also tended to rip the packaging when pulled off, which annoyed gift givers. And then there is the issue of inventory "shrinkage," as it's called in the industry. When a store puts all its stock out on display, a few items inevitably somehow make it out the door without going to the cashier first.

With the clipboard model, we displayed samples in the showroom of merchandise that was immediately available in a warehouse attached to each store. That way the customers could see and experience what they would be getting from our catalog, but they wouldn't have to carry it around the store while shopping. Instead, they would carry a clipboard with an order form. If they wanted to buy an item on display, they would write down the stock number on the order form. Some merchandise remained self-service—primarily toys and sporting goods—and salespeople would assist shoppers at our jewelry counter and in our "sight and sound" department where we sold cameras and record players and such.

When ready to check out, the customer would take the order form to the service counter, where an associate would send it via pneumatic tube to our warehouse. The warehouse staff would quickly pull the order and place the product on a conveyor belt to deliver it out to the merchandise pickup area on the sales floor and complete the purchase. Originally, the stores had separate pay areas for clipboard sales and self-service items and jewelry, but later, with computerized registers, we were able to consolidate the purchases for the customers' convenience.

Installing those conveyor belts and pneumatic tubes was a major undertaking but well worth it. The clipboard model streamlined our order process. We only had to ticket the samples on display in the showroom, not the entire inventory back in the warehouse. And we gained better control over our inventory. No longer did we have to bulk out the showroom shelves. The customer expected to see only the single sample and didn't know or care whether we had one or fifty in the back, so long as we fulfilled the order. Generally, they already knew what they wanted when they came into the store; they had made their selections at home while browsing the catalog and arrived with a list. That was why it was crucial that we kept an accurate inventory and stocked everything in that catalog. A store didn't need to stock multiples of an item if it was likely to sell only one every three months. And with only a fraction of the inventory out in the showroom, the shrinkage problem shrunk.

Meanwhile, back in the warehouse, the employees were trained on fulfillment practices. They knew where everything was kept so they could get it onto the conveyor without delay, and if an item needed to be shipped to a customer's home, they knew how to pack it appropriately and efficiently. That was their job. The warehouse associates didn't need to double as salespeople, and vice versa.

We didn't invent the clipboard system any more than we invented the catalog showroom concept. Best Products and most of the others in our catalog group already were using clipboards, and we learned from what they were experiencing. Our mutual respect for the Lewis family that operated Best Products had grown as we observed each other at meetings where members of the Creative Merchandising group weighed in on catalog selections. Best Products had computer records to back up its choices. We had records, too, although ours initially were manual. The other members showed up without records.

As we became friendly with the Lewises, they helped us to transition to the clipboards. We sent people out to Richmond to study their operation. "We want to do whatever they're doing," I said. "If they stick a pole in the middle of their floor, we'll stick a pole in the middle of our floor." We wanted to get our system up and running so that we could evaluate which aspects would work best for us. As we grew, we carefully observed how others in the industry did things and often found them to be generous in sharing what they had learned.

The innovation paid off well both in sales and in customer satisfaction. Every store we converted to clipboard sales showed a dramatic increase in sales. Same with our new acquisitions; we introduced clipboards and conveyors to most of those stores, and each of them saw sales skyrocketing. Our customers were pleased. Today, as they look back fondly on the many years they shopped at Service Merchandise, they often emphasize how much they enjoyed watching their order coming down that conveyor belt, usually within minutes.

THE P15 PERCOLATOR

For years, General Electric made a percolator, Model P15, that never changed much. Service Merchandise carried it from beginning to end. And for years, whenever I would give a speech to analysts or shareholders, I would talk about that percolator. I pointed it out as a shining example of the consistency of our merchandise from year to year.

"You've made that percolator famous!" my colleagues told me. And so, all right, I'll accept some of the credit. But it couldn't have happened if General Electric hadn't introduced that classic coffeemaker and recognized there's no need to mess with a good thing.

A Technological Edge

While the customers were enjoying this fun and novel way to shop, I was having nightmares about situations that could develop. I imagined, for example, this scenario:

It's the Saturday before Christmas, and we're abundantly busy—a happy time but hectic. To keep the cash registers from overflowing, we are doing cash pickups every few hours. A few minutes before noon, a customer writes us a check, and at the noon pickup, that check gets swept off to the counting room. Meanwhile, she's watching the conveyor, eager for her purchase to arrive—but it doesn't. The warehouse informs the service counter at 12:03 p.m. that the item has sold out. Not only do we have a disappointed customer, but, on the busiest day of the year, we're keeping her waiting while we devote time that we can't spare to hunting down her check and issuing a refund.

To avoid such a mess, what we needed was inventory control that was as accurate as humanly possible—and, with the development of increasingly sophisticated technology, even better than humanly possible. We needed a modern, computerized system that was up to the challenge of supporting the growth that we envisioned.

We proceeded to develop an inventory management system that was years ahead of its time. Doing so required the devotion of a lot of talented folks. Technology without people is pointless. Someone needed to coordinate our efforts, and I was the human who did it. I became, in effect, the interpreter between our IT people and the store managers and buyers—the "doers" and the "users" of the technology. I didn't have a clue how to program a computer, but I knew how to keep everybody communicating.

We assembled a top-notch IT team, which was unusual for most companies at the time. The managers and buyers knew what they wanted, which wasn't necessarily what they needed. The techs knew what was possible, at least for the moment. As for me, I knew what would be best for our business, and I tried to keep everyone working toward ambitious goals. I would meet in my office every Saturday morning with the IT team and some of the store managers and outline what we expected our system to accomplish—and by the next Wednesday, the testing complete, we would decide whether we were ready to roll out our innovations to the chain.

By the mid-1970s, we had converted all our company showrooms to point-of-sale electronic cash registers. Each showroom had an on-site computer that transmitted information over the telephone lines to our headquarters in Nashville.

In designing that point-of-sale system, we focused on the product code that was on the merchandise packaging. It was unique to every item. Could that be an alternative to putting a price tag on each product? Wouldn't that be better than relying on the cashier or customer to get the correct information? We needed sophisticated equipment that could read the letters and numbers of that code, assign a price to it, and track the sales for accurate inventory.

No such equipment was yet available, though, at anything close to affordable. Honeywell was beginning to develop systems with the potential we needed. The company had designed a small computer that could process information from several sales terminals, but it was prohibitively expensive. We ended up hiring the Honeywell salesman to find a computer that would serve our needs. With his help, our team designed a system that combined parts from unrelated devices. We put together a computer screen, printer, and cash drawer, and we linked it to a minicomputer that, eventually, could handle a dozen registers in a store.

We invested heavily in that technology so that we could get one of those systems in each of our stores—and as a result, we were able to track our inventory in real time. We had exact numbers of what had been sold and when. Later, when we were able to transmit via satellite dish instead of phone lines, the process got faster and cheaper. Every store could share its sales figures and inventory every fifteen minutes. And as the microprocessors improved, the system could handle thirty-six registers in a store.

From the start, we employed the power of technology. We understood that what we really were investing in was customer service. We wanted the best for our shoppers because the best is what would keep them coming back. In time, for example, the clipboards and pneumatic tubes would give way to computer kiosks. Instead of filling out a slip, the shopper could key in a selection, swipe a credit card, and take the receipt directly to the conveyor area—where the item already might be waiting. The customer's order went directly from kiosk to warehouse. This was our "Silent Sam" system.

Simply Jewelry

During all those growth years, our business model remained simple. Whether the store was in Omaha or Tallahassee or Bangor, the inventory was much the same, and it sold at the same price. There wasn't much difference in what sold in which regions—with a few exceptions. And one of those exceptions was jewelry, which was simply the most important part of our business.

All in all, we knew what to expect any time of year. Christmas came at the same time every winter. So did Valentine's Day and Mother's Day. All we had to do was make sure we had the right inventory in stock for the current catalog season. We had learned that the summer clearances should start on the Fourth of July in every store, no matter where. When we entered the Miami market, we figured that summer goods would sell year-round there. We shipped loads of lawn furniture to Miami, hoping to sell it without a markdown (because isn't it always summer in southern Florida?). Didn't matter. On the fifth of July, the market for lawn furniture is just as dead in Miami as it is in the North.

It's not that we ignored regional differences and demographics, of course. You don't need much insight, for example, to realize you won't sell many riding mowers in downtown Chicago. No reason to stock those there. And we learned something interesting about electric blankets, which were popular on chilly winter nights in the South where many homes aren't well insulated. We figured they'd be a hot seller when we opened in Chicago, so we loaded that store with them. After all, the winters there are cold and windy, right? I visited that store the following January and saw electric blankets stacked to the ceiling. "They're not selling very well," the store manager told me. "See, folks up here keep their homes toasty. They've got good heating systems and plenty of insulation."

Our jewelry departments showed some of the biggest regional differences. In the South, for example, customers wanted yellow gold. In the North, they favored white gold. About a dozen of our stores sold high-end jewelry in greater volume than the others, so we stocked accordingly. Nobody wanted costume or faux jewelry, though. We tested both, but our customers were clear that they wanted the real thing. They desired the gold and the diamonds.

In some markets, customers shopping for a diamond ring would prefer a one-carat solitaire; in other markets, the customers would want a one-carat cluster. The reason? The solitaire sold for, say, $2,000. But a cluster of ten stones totaling a carat sold for perhaps half that price. The demographics, including income levels, determined the preference. We made sure each store had one of each kind of ring, and when it sold, we shipped in another immediately to replace it.

Jewelry was at the center of our sales—and we featured it prominently in the center of our showrooms. At the jewelry counter, customers got one-on-one service from a sales associate. The jewelry didn't come down the conveyor belt. By the mid-1970s, jewelry was accounting for a quarter of our sales volume, though it only took up a small fraction of the square footage in our stores.

We had the distinction of becoming the nation's largest retailer of watches, and no other company sold more jewelry under one name. That fact led me to shrug at market research that suggested our shoppers weren't particularly interested in our jewelry. How, then, were we selling so much? Market research also informed us that people didn't care for our conveyor belts, but as folks today reminisce about our stores, it's the conveyor belts that they often mention first.

Despite our success as a jewelry merchant, Daddy didn't want "Service Merchandise" to appear on the boxes in which the diamonds and other pieces were sold. He didn't want to remind people where they might return their purchase. "We guarantee the diamond, not the romance," he liked to say—and though romances often end, we hoped our sales were forever.

In the late 1970s, when the price of gold spiked to several times its previous value, we faced a big question—and it was the same one that others in the catalog industry were asking. The catalogs had been published months earlier, with the jewelry prices listed. Do you raise those prices or honor the price in the catalog? We chose to honor the advertised price, even for the end-of-the-year shopping season.

Our jewelry sales played another key role: they allowed us to sell other merchandise in our stores at lower prices. We favored merchandise of upper or at least standard quality, because that's what our customers wanted. However, we could sell standard-quality items for the same price that discounters sold the low-end stuff. And we could sell our high-end merchandise for the price that the department stores sold the standard goods. Our great prices brought a lot of traffic to our stores—and generated a lot of jewelry sales when people came in. That's where we made money. Our profits were in the jewelry, and they allowed us to sell the rest at lower markups.

A few years after gold prices began spiking, we opened a New York jewelry office. We felt confident that we could reduce costs and provide better quality for our customers by contracting with the various vendors typically involved in producing an item of jewelry—the diamond and stone dealers, the casters, the setters, the polishers, and such. One of our diamond vendors, M. Fabrikant & Sons, gave us corner space in their building for our office—a remarkably generous gesture, considering that we would be doing business with competing vendors. We believed we could accomplish those manufacturing tasks far more economically and pass the savings on to our shoppers. Eventually we moved from that corner office to a much larger space in New York and functioned as a jewelry distribution center, where we would do quality control, warehousing, and distribution to the stores.

Daddy wasn't doing all that to make extra money ... he did it to pass on better value to our customers.

This was another brilliant move by my father, who simply loved jewelry, though he hadn't been in the jewelry business before we got into catalog sales. He had a knack for envisioning how to create beautiful pieces at reasonable costs.

He worked with the designers, for example, to produce those diamond cluster rings. They were the same carat weight as a solitaire and just as lovely, or lovelier, but you didn't have to pay so dearly for them. He understood that a forty-point diamond in the center of that cluster was indistinguishable from a fifty-point stone yet significantly less expensive. And he knew that the customers cared more about that setting than how much gold was in the shank that went around the finger. He could make that thinner to help bring down the cost.

Daddy wasn't doing all that to make extra money, though. He did it to pass on better value to our customers—and that culture, in many ways, defined Service Merchandise.

A TOUCH OF JACK DANIELS

Developing relationships had much to do with our success—and sometimes that can be as simple as spending a day at a distillery.

For years, we had been frustrated in our desire for Service Merchandise to become an official distributor of Seiko watches and have a consistent supply for our customers. One year, I went to Japan with several colleagues to visit jewelry vendors, and primarily Seiko. We took a senior executive from the company out to dinner at a French restaurant. He spoke virtually no English and seemed sullen, but he clearly was enjoying the meal and drinks.

I noted that he had a taste for Jack Daniels. "Next time you come to the States," I told him through his interpreter, "I'm going to take you to the Jack Daniels distillery."

He nodded enthusiastically and grinned. It was the first smile I'd seen on his face.

The next year at the jewelry show in New York, I walked into the Seiko booth, and that same executive was there. He recognized me at once.

"Jack Daniels," he said. "Jack Daniels!"

I arranged a date to send a plane to bring him to Nashville, and then a group of us took him down to Miss Bobo's Boarding House and Restaurant, near Lynchburg, Tennessee, where he filled up on pork chops, lima beans, and turnip greens. Then we took him on a VIP tour of the distillery, where he had ample opportunity to sample the product. Afterward he posed proudly with us for a group photo at a sculpture of Jack Daniels.

Four months later, at the spring jewelry show, I again visited the Seiko booth. This time, he greeted me with a rush of enthusiasm, though I didn't understand a word he said. I turned to his interpreter. "He says that was such a delightful visit with you," the interpreter said, "and you're going to be our new distributor!"

"Boss Man's in the Building!"

Throughout the year, I would spend much of my time—a few days a week on average—visiting the stores in our growing network, at first traveling by car, later by plane. I felt that the company leaders needed to demonstrate to the store associates that we cared, and I often traveled with district and regional managers. Sometimes we would travel to five cities a day, using five rental cars.

If we arrived late at night, we would look for a hotel near the store. "Before we check in," I would say, "let's drive over and see what it's like behind the warehouse and do a cruise through the parking lot." I wanted to see how well the premises were maintained. Had any trash been left out? If I saw any carts still in the lot, I put my business card on them.

Unlike the others in our entourage, I generally didn't go straight to the store manager on those visits. Instead, I would stop by the warehouse. How efficiently was it operating? How well was it organized? How accurate was the inventory? I would just walk in— and if nobody questioned my presence, that was another issue. While I was there, I would pitch in to fill orders as they came off the printer. I wasn't asking anyone to do anything that I wouldn't do, though I drew the line when I tried to load a set of barbells.

During a visit to a Florida store a week before Christmas, I headed to the warehouse and passed a wall phone that the employees used. It rang. Nobody was nearby, so I answered.

"Hello?" I said.

"Listen, the big boss man's in the building. Be cool!"

"Where are you?" I asked.

"I'm on the dock. Be cool. He's here!"

"Yes, he is!" I said. "And he's coming over now to see you."

I confess. I enjoyed moments like that. I loved that element of surprise. And I enjoyed teaching moments. Driving down Interstate 24 one day, while on an outing with my daughter Robyn and four of her friends, I tried to pass one of our delivery trucks—but the driver kept blocking me. I got on the CB radio.

"Hey, Service Merchandise, where're you heading?"

"On my way to Chattanooga."

"Would that be store number five or store number seven?"

"Huh? Who is this anyway? How do you know those numbers?"

"Just guessing, good buddy."

The kids burst out laughing.

That trucker must have told someone at the store about that odd snippet of conversation because within a few days the story was relayed to me. "Yeah, I know about it because that was me on the CB," I said.

The next day the trucker called me to apologize.

"I'm not looking for an apology," I told him. "But let me just ask: Why couldn't you have been nice and let me pass? That truck says *Service Merchandise* in big letters, and anyone you treat like that is going to think we're not a very nice company. This isn't about me. It's about us."

Whenever I was about to pay a visit to a store, the staff often would somehow figure out that I was coming. Once, flying home from Mexico, I looked down and saw the lights of Laredo, Texas. "Could you circle back and land?" I asked the pilot. "I want to see how our new store here is doing." The store was on a street parallel to the runway, so I strolled right over—and the employees were lined up waiting for me. "How did you know I'd be here?" I asked. "It was just fifteen minutes ago that I decided to come." Word gets out.

I learned more in surprise visits than in announced ones—although, through the years, I met a colleague or two who felt it was disrespectful to just show up without warning. I never understood that. I figured we needed to see what the stores really looked like, not what they were supposed to look like.

When I visited one of our stores in New York, for example, I saw a line of customers in the showroom waiting for their merchandise. What was up with that? I hurried over to the warehouse, where I saw a six-foot-five kid filling the orders—or rather, not filling the orders. He was just sort of moping around. I began hustling to get the items on the conveyor, and he picked up his pace. We didn't stop until we were caught up.

"Do you play sports?" I asked, looking up at him.

"Yessir. Basketball."

"Are you any good?"

"Well, I made all-city honorable mention."

"But are you pro?"

"No, no way. I'm still in high school. Why are you asking?"

"Because if you're going to be really good at basketball, or at anything, you've got to hustle. And so here I'm paying you, but from what I see, you haven't been hustling very much." I told him who I was, and he was too astonished to say anything.

"Look," I said. "Do you want to be lifting boxes the rest of your life? If you hustle, you could have a shot at running this warehouse. Or running this store. Or you could work your way up to a job like mine. But you can't get ahead in life by moping around."

The young man started to cry. Another teaching moment—but I hadn't meant to bring him to tears.

"What's your name?" I asked softly.

"Smitty," he said, wiping his eyes. "Nobody's ever told me stuff like that," he said. "Nobody's ever talked to me like that."

Several months later, during a conference with the store manager, I inquired about Smitty. "How's he doing?"

"Smitty? Wow. I don't know what you did," the manager said, "but that guy really moves. In fact, he's so good that I'm thinking of bringing him out to the sales floor."

People aren't machines. You don't just wind them up and set them to work. They need to hear the "why" of what you expect them to do. They deserve to know the significance of their role and how their job could play into their future. And they deserved to hear the truth about how they were performing. If someone clearly lacked potential to grow with us, my philosophy was to act sooner rather than later. Sometimes it's best to just let people get on with life.

We strived to place our associates in positions where they could do well. We had assistant managers who excelled and earned a promotion to manager—but couldn't handle that level. That didn't mean we fired them. We put them back to where they were doing a good job. Why should we let Target or Walmart get a good assistant that we had trained? Sometimes, an employee would try out a new job, then ask to be demoted. We had no problem with that.

We always played to our people's strengths. They understood from their first day on the job that they could rise as far as they wished. As they witnessed how fast we were growing, they had every reason to believe the promotions would come swiftly. Instead of bringing in outsiders, we chose from among our best. We made it worth their while to stick around. And we accepted those who didn't wish to join the ranks of management, so long as they were doing their job responsibly. Not everyone wants to climb the ladder—but those who did could feel reassured that they wouldn't get stranded up there.

NURTURING A PRECIOUS ASSET

I wanted our people to think, to be creative, to come up with ideas that would make our operations better than ever. When given that freedom, they often came through. And when they did, we made sure they got the recognition they deserved.

One evening, I stopped at one of our stores in Maine and chatted with the manager on duty. He had been on the job only three weeks, which meant he still had a fresh perspective. "Tell me anything you think is wrong with this store," I said. He was caught off guard but did offer that he felt the store office and the conveyor belt could be located more efficiently.

The next day, I dropped in at the store as the managers were holding a planning meeting. "So what are you planning on changing?" I asked, and they mentioned paint colors but not much else. "Well, okay, so I guess you guys are right on it," I said, and I left.

A few hours later, one of the store's top managers approached me. "You must have had something in mind," he said. "What is it that *you* want to change?"

I mentioned the conveyor belt and office. "Are you sure they're in the right place?"

At the next planning session, I explained the rationale for moving them.

"Great idea," they said.

And then I told them it wasn't my idea. "It was your new guy out there on the floor who brought that up with me when I asked for his thoughts," I said. "See, I don't work here in this store, but you all do, so you're the ones who need to keep thinking how to do things better and better."

I was gruff at times. I was known for my short fuse. A department manager of diminutive stature once tried to tell me he wasn't attending to a line of customers because he hadn't noticed that they were there. I hoisted him up by his armpits: "There! Can you see them *now*?" Another time, a manager was chatting with me about how much she loved to cook. "Well don't ever invite me for dinner," I told her, "because I wouldn't want to eat if your kitchen is as filthy as the way you keep this department."

I'm not proud of exchanges like that. I'd rather think of my kindnesses, but it was all part of the package of who I am. I expected our associates to do their very best and wanted them to think for themselves. If one store had a sales display at the front and another store that was virtually identical had it in the back, I asked why. Which was right, and which was wrong?

Which would bring the greater volume? Over and over I asked questions like that.

Through the years, we found numerous ways to honor and encourage our people. I signed personal letters to employees who had contributed to our phenomenal growth. We had an employee incentive department devoted to giving out awards—pins and watches and even diamond jewelry for exemplary sales. We gave bonuses to employees who sold the most "green tag" merchandise that we needed to move on clearance. Not only did we have company-wide incentives, but each store and district also added their own initiatives to bolster retention and morale.

We recognized that our employees were our most precious asset. We also highly valued our vendors, because without them we would have had no merchandise—and without any merchandise, we would have had no customers, no sales, no business. I'm sure our customers appreciated our devotion to them, but they also expected us to stock the things they wanted to buy.

A Remarkable Decade

By the turn of the decade, we began printing our own catalog. The industry was hotter than ever, and some major players like Grants and Giant Food and others were getting into the business. *What would we do,* we wondered, *if a competitor such as Kmart purchased Modern Merchandising, whose Creative division published our catalog? Would the new owner cut us out of the deal and leave us without a catalog?* We couldn't risk that. The catalog was our lifeblood.

As Service Merchandise grew, we were running out of places to put stores where others weren't using the same catalog. When we went into new areas, we would at least try to buy the other businesses. We didn't want to jeopardize store owners with whom we were friendly and who used the same catalog that we did. Our solution was to begin publishing our own catalog, avoiding that conflict. The bottom line is that we needed to maintain control over our own destiny.

Once we began publishing our own catalog, we felt more freedom to enter markets where others in the industry already were operating. Richmond, for example. When the mother of one of our department heads died, several of us flew to her funeral in Richmond, where she lived. We were in a company plane, and after we landed, an airport employee whose husband worked at Best Products called him to say a Service Merchandise team had come to town. The news soon went out over a loudspeaker at the company's headquarters. It seems our presence caused a panic: *Just what are they doing in Richmond?*

No, we weren't trying to lay siege on Richmond. What we were doing, overall, was concluding a remarkable decade of growth as we headed into the 1980s. Our simplicity was one of our great strengths. Operating a Service Merchandise store was much different from operating a Kmart or Walmart or Target. We had salespeople in select departments, but other than that, we needed only those samples on display in the showroom. We didn't need to continually reorganize the sales floor and restock shelves.

We were able to expand so effectively because we had associates who were extraordinary at their jobs, whether that was setting up the new stores, staffing them, or operating the sales floor. Each of those associates contributed essential expertise needed to build such an enterprise. At every level, our people served with dedication—to be the best they could be. We could be tough, but we were honest and fair and professional. We treated people well. To this day, those who served together still recall their respect and admiration for one another, both on the job and off. We were colleagues, and we were friends. None of us could have done it alone—but by putting our heads together, we made it happen.

THE SPLITTING DIFFERENCE

One of the tricks that I discovered in our early days as a public company was how to use a stock split to our advantage. I developed a theory on how we could use those splits to keep our stock prices rising.

Our concern was that investors who wanted a piece of the big three in the catalog showroom industry would choose either Modern Merchandising or Best Products instead of us. Why? Best Products had the advantage of trading on the New York Stock Exchange, not over the counter like Modern Merchandising and us. And Modern had the advantage of being the publisher of the catalog that we all used.

So where did that leave Service Merchandise in investors' eyes? I figured the solution would be to adjust what those eyes perceived.

I began with the premise that it is highly unlikely that the stock of any company, unless it totally dominates its field, will sell for both a higher price per share and a have higher P/E (or price-earnings ratio). One or the other, but rarely both.

Because we had close ties with the folks from both Modern and Best Products, we all knew what the others would be posting for their earnings. With that knowledge, our company could do whatever it took to offer investors a bargain price for our shares while also showing a higher P/E. Every year, we could do a two-for-one stock split, for example, or a three-for-two.

Let's say a company is worth a million dollars and has a million shares outstanding at a dollar a share. In a two-to-one split, it would have two million shares outstanding at fifty cents a share. It's still a million-dollar company, but the stock sells at half the price. In other words, with a stock split, we could give investors more shares at a lower price with the same value as fewer shares at a higher price.

I was convinced that investors would buy price—and that the demand would drive growth. A stock selling for $5, for example, would grow to $7.50 faster than a stock selling for $10 would rise to $15. That's a 50 percent gain for each, but the less expensive stock reaches the goal sooner.

That was my theory. And that is what happened every year that we did a stock split. People would see that we had a lower price and a higher P/E than either Best Products or Modern Merchandising. That is how we convinced investors that they should put their money on us. All in all, we seemed the better bet.

Zimmerman's Five and Ten Cent Store - Pulaski, TN

*Harry Zimmerman in Naval
uniform 1943–1945*

*Raymond with his two younger sisters
Sue (left) and Doris (right)*

First Service Merchandise Store in Nashville, TN
on Broadway downtown

Alice, Raymond, Mary, Henry, Sue, and Doris
Zimmerman - 1960s

Mary and Harry Zimmerman - 1960s

Robyn Zimmerman Rubinoff and Fred Zimmerman
circa 1971

Harry and Mary Zimmerman - 1980s

Harry Zimmerman at MDA Telethon with Jerry Lewis

Raymond Zimmerman with MDA poster child - 1995

Raymond Zimmerman with Golda Meir,
Israeli Prime Minister - 1974

$3.00

Everybody's Everyday Gift Store

AMERICA'S LEADING JEWELER

Service

MERCHANDISE

1994/1995 Jewelry And General Merchandise Catalog

Service Merchandise catalog - 1994–1995

Proud associates at a store opening

Service Merchandise Store

Associate name tags

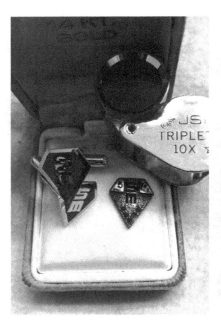

*Sales associates' loyalty and incentive
awards and pins*

Associate recognition watch

*Jewelry
Department*

*Gift
Department*

*Sight and Sound
Department*

*Toy
Department*

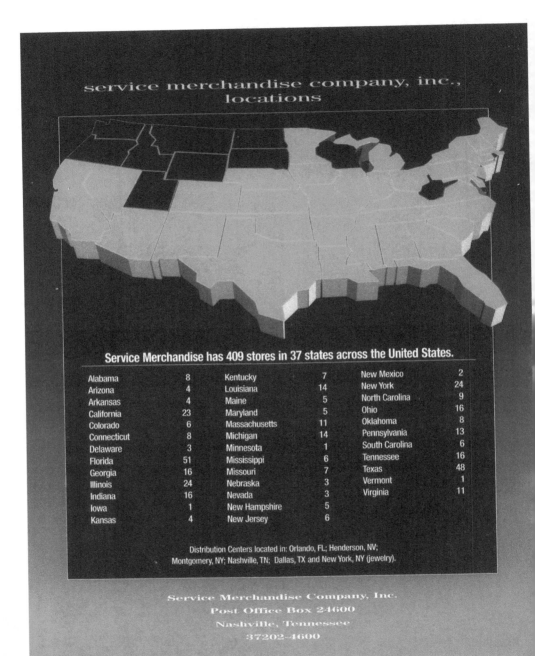

service merchandise company, inc., locations

Service Merchandise has 409 stores in 37 states across the United States.

Alabama	8	Kentucky	7	New Mexico	2
Arizona	4	Louisiana	14	New York	24
Arkansas	4	Maine	5	North Carolina	9
California	23	Maryland	5	Ohio	16
Colorado	6	Massachusetts	11	Oklahoma	8
Connecticut	8	Michigan	14	Pennsylvania	13
Delaware	3	Minnesota	1	South Carolina	6
Florida	51	Mississippi	6	Tennessee	16
Georgia	16	Missouri	7	Texas	48
Illinois	24	Nebraska	3	Vermont	1
Indiana	16	Nevada	3	Virginia	11
Iowa	1	New Hampshire	5		
Kansas	4	New Jersey	6		

Distribution Centers located in: Orlando, FL; Henderson, NV;
Montgomery, NY; Nashville, TN; Dallas, TX and New York, NY (jewelry).

Service Merchandise Company, Inc.
Post Office Box 24600
Nashville, Tennessee
37202-4600

Service Merchandise store map 1995

The INDY Car with Willy T. Ribbs and Raymond Zimmerman

Price sign at 99 cents

Raymond at the 99 Cent Stuff store

*A family affair—volunteering at the
community Thanksgiving*

*Robyn Rubinoff and Fred Zimmerman
at the community Thanksgiving*

Community Thanksgiving with over 700 guests

Etta and Raymond Zimmerman

*From right to left—Max Rubinoff, Raymond holding Theo Kaufman,
Sam Rubinoff holding Ezra Kaufman*

The Zimmerman family

Raymond and his sister Sue Kresge 2021

It's the 1980s ...

- The internet and mobile phones are beginning to change lives.

- The AIDS crisis spreads worldwide.

- CD players make their debut.

- The Berlin Wall falls, signaling the end of the Cold War.

  ... and Service Merchandise sees soaring growth.

Through the Years ...

- 1981: Raymond Zimmerman becomes chairman, president, and CEO.

- 1980–85: Specialty stores sell toys, computers, hardware, lingerie, and jewelry.

- 1986: Harry and Mary Zimmerman pass away.

- 1987: The company begins an annual black-tie dinner, a fundraiser for MDA.

- 1989: Service Merchandise pays out a ten-dollar-a-share dividend.

- 1989: The company caps the decade with 334 stores and $3.3 billion in sales.

CHAPTER 5

Prime Time, 1980–1990

THE 1980S WAS a decade of surging growth for Service Merchandise. We tripled our number of stores and our earnings. Our sales quadrupled. But amid those go-go years came a huge loss—the death of my parents. They had come into this world in 1911 within a few months of each other, and so, too, did they leave. Daddy passed on in the summer of '86. Mother waited only till fall. They lie together now in Nashville.

At the time of his death, the Muscular Dystrophy Association in Nashville had been planning a fundraising dinner at which Daddy was to be the honoree, in recognition of his years of inspirational work for MDA. The association proceeded with the affair, dedicating it to his memory. Hundreds attended, and we decided that Service Merchandise would turn it into a tradition. For years afterward, we sponsored a black-tie dinner and a two-day fundraiser at the Opryland Hotel in Nashville.

After the Jerry Lewis telethons began in the midsixties on Labor Day weekends, my father appeared regularly on the national broadcasts to present donations to the MDA. When he died, he was the organization's national vice president. After his death, I would represent our company at the telethons. Service Merchandise established itself as a major corporate benefactor in fighting the disease.

Philanthropy became a hallmark of our family, company, and associates, and Daddy and Mother were the heart of it. They taught my sisters and me how to live right. They set the tone, and their example was a joy to maintain. It was a major part of their legacy and the Service Merchandise company culture. Such corporate outreach wasn't common at the time. We became a trendsetter.

> *Philanthropy became a hallmark of our family, company, and associates, and Daddy and Mother were the heart of it.*

I am proud of the selfless spirit that led our greater family—our vendors, our employees, our customers—to contribute so much to that effort. Our vendors were the major donors at our annual fundraisers, and most of the $3 million that we raised each year for MDA came from that event. Each year about two thousand attended, participating in a golf tournament and casino night. Those two days became an industry-wide social event at which vendors and buyers gathered for a great cause.

Often, the MDA poster child of the year would attend the fundraising dinner. It was pure joy to witness the smile on that little one's face upon seeing all the love in the room. Every year, people were becoming increasingly aware of a disease that so long was in the shadows. Humanity still awaits a cure, despite the progress, but every donated dollar purchased hope—and that made it all worthwhile.

Though the MDA drive was the focus of Service Merchandise's philanthropy, we supported communities in a variety of other ways. We gave each of our stores a budget of funds to give away to local nonprofits. Our employees also contributed generously to United Way. I was determined that every year, in every store, a representative from the organization should pay a visit to our associates to explain in detail who benefits from the donations and the services that they provide to the community. To me, getting out the word was the most important aspect of the United Way campaigns. I wanted our people to be well versed on their options if they found themselves in need.

We also participated regularly in the PENCIL foundation, which helps Nashville schools and students by rallying community resources to provide supplies, tutoring, mentoring, and more. Daddy was very active in funding day camp programs for the blind and visually impaired. We supported the Big Brothers Big Sisters youth-mentoring program as well.

Our objective was the betterment of the communities that we served. I encouraged our senior managers to serve on the boards of philanthropic organizations, the symphony, and performing arts groups. I wanted them to enrich their lives and spread the message of our mission. In those and other ways, we encouraged our associates to become involved with the community. At the time, it was an unusual and progressive approach. I felt that people who care about the welfare of others would be the best fit for our company culture.

Service Merchandise also encouraged customers to contribute. Once, as I paid an anonymous visit to a store and posed as a customer, an associate approached me on the sales floor. "Would you like to buy a candy bar for the Muscular Dystrophy Association?" he asked. The store manager was nearby and could hear our conversation.

I decided to have a little fun. "Not now," I said, as I feigned intense interest in a camera that was for sale.

"That's okay, sir," he said. "But, you know, it's for such a good cause."

"That's nice. I'm glad you're doing that, but I don't want a candy bar," I said. "I might want to buy this camera, though."

"Okay, well, if you change your mind, we have a donation box over there by the checkout," the associate said. "We're hoping to give—"

"Look. *Please* just tell me about this camera," I said gruffly. The young man immediately put on his sales hat and began to detail all the features—and then the store manager turned, recognized me, and apologized profusely.

"That's okay," I said, grinning. I patted the associate's shoulder. "Give this fellow a gold star. Not only does he know cameras, but he knows what we're all about."

I give full credit to my parents for making it clear what we were all about. They established in our company a spirit of unity. They never argued. If they disagreed on anything significant, I never knew about it because they always spoke with a common voice about the directions we should take and what we stood for. I had the honor of working side by side with them for forty-five years. Our company and our family were privileged to have them at the helm all those years. Such leadership is rare.

As I was writing these words, my phone rang. It was the son of a gentleman with whom we did business long ago. "I wanted you to know," he said, "that my father died yesterday." He was ninety-eight.

Afterward, my first thought was that I wished I could call Daddy. I wanted to tell him about it, the way we once told each other about everything under the sun. I wanted to let him know that our old friend was gone—but I suspect, by then, he already knew.

"The way I see it," Daddy would have corrected me, "it's not that he's gone but that he's arrived."

It's going on four decades since my parents passed, and I still miss the sound of their voices. They spoke truth into so many lives, and through their life's work in business and philanthropy, they built a family of many thousands who hold them in high esteem to this day.

Thriving amid Change

As the catalog showroom industry advanced into the 1980s, the retail landscape was changing. Big-box competitors and warehouse clubs were making their appearance. Our strategy, in part, was to shift increasingly to more upscale merchandise while also watching the retail market for opportunities to diversify our operations and adjust to the trends. In short, we upped our game and enjoyed some of our best years. All along, we maintained the attention to our customers that had sown our success. Year after year, we continued to expand with record-breaking performance.

Our sales grew powerfully, passing $1 billion in 1981 and well over $3 billion by the end of the decade. We began the 1980s with 101 stores and ended with 334. We continued a strategy that we began in the 1970s of placing mini showrooms (30,000 square feet) in less populated areas to attract folks who weren't likely to drive to our larger urban locations. The aim was to get closer to the customers.

My father retired in 1981, continuing as honorary chairman and company director. I assumed the posts of chairman, president, and CEO. Meanwhile, we began to relocate our corporate headquarters from our four main facilities in the city of Nashville. Over the course of several years, we consolidated our headquarters under one roof in Brentwood, ten miles to the south.

In 1982, we purchased the Sam Solomon Company, a catalog showroom operator based in Charleston, South Carolina, and added its seven outlets to our holdings. We drove a hard deal, and afterward Melvin Solomon, a wonderful man, sent me a letter along with a little package. "I had to visit my dentist today," he wrote, "so I figured you might as well get these too." Inside the box were two teeth.

That same year, we also tried to acquire Modern Merchandising, whose publishing division for years had produced our catalog until we began printing our own. Best Products, which also had been in that catalog group, outbid us for the deal. Though we lost out on that merger, we continued to make a variety of other acquisitions.

In our use of technology, we continued to break ground. During the first few years of the decade, we launched the first version of our "Silent Sam" system (which we later renamed Service Express) by which shoppers could visit a store kiosk to check inventory and reserve the items that they wished to buy. They could make a purchase directly at the kiosk and then go directly to the conveyor belt for pickup. It was a creative use of computer technology that reassured customers that we had what they wanted in stock. Silent Sam was the result of our people thinking outside the box.

We also developed a computer program that could zero in on demographics to help predict market trends with remarkable accuracy, and we set up a computerized inventory replenishment system. With cool and efficient calculations, it kept track of which merchandise needed to be shipped to where and when and how much should be purchased to keep us in stock and our customers happy. Our buyers could confidently order an initial distribution of merchandise among the stores based on demographics and trends from earlier catalog sales, and then the computer took over from there, redistributing and reordering automatically as necessary. Technology was central to our growth. With so many stores, computers did a far better job of ordering and tracking merchandise than we could ever have managed to do manually. The computers helped our company deliver the great service that our very name promised.

My personal life also was changing. During a trip to Israel as the decade began, I met Arlene, who would become my second wife. We spent fourteen happy years together traveling and enjoying time with our families.

Along the Way

In the early years of the 1980s, we made several efforts to diversify with specialty stores and chains, in markets around the country. We opened stores specializing in toys, home improvement and hardware, computers, jewelry, and lingerie. None came close to the surging revenues of our catalog showrooms. In the end, we concluded that we served our customers best by staying on the path that had brought us success. A great company requires more than passion; it requires a dedication to its core business model. Those sidelines, however, are part of our company's history. Even if they didn't grow our bottom line, we certainly grew from the experience—and we met a lot of fine folks along the way.

The Toy Store

In 1980, the Lionel toy-store chain announced that it would be opening in Nashville and Louisville, at locations near our stores. I had long been interested in opening a toy store, and it seemed the time was right to make that move. I needed to see how a modern toy store operated, so I assembled a team of twelve and sent them out to half a dozen Toys "R" Us locations. "I want to know every item they've got and where they put it on the shelf—and get the prices, too, because we want to sell at the same price."

Two days later, I answered my phone. It was a top executive of Toys "R" Us, and he wasn't happy.

"What's the matter?" I asked.

"You know what's the matter," he said flatly. "Get your people out of our stores."

I didn't have a clue what to say, but my mouth kept going. "Oh! Well, hey, we just want to be like you when we grow up—"

"Raymond! Get ... your ... people ... out ... of ... our ... stores."

It seems my surveillance crew roved around snapping photographs and stretching tape measures up and down the displays. They weren't exactly subtle. Nonetheless, we did our best to mirror that model, starting in Louisville and Nashville and eventually expanding to six locations. Choosing a name for our toy store had been tough. We considered several ideas. "Hey, let's call it The Toy Store," someone finally suggested in a stroke of brilliance.

After two years, our toy-store story was done. The stores required a dedicated inventory to sell year-round, but it didn't make sense to stack up hot toys in a warehouse when our Service Merchandise stores needed the inventory for the holidays and could easily sell them in a day. In hindsight, we didn't put the right management in place. A familiar lesson: It's all about the people.

The Computer Shoppe

By the 1980s, anyone whose eyes were half open could see that computers would be increasingly central to our society's functions. The personal-home-computer market was booming, and our company didn't want to miss out.

In 1983, we acquired a three-store chain in Nashville called the Computer Shoppe. We had been selling the popular Atari video game consoles in our stores, but we wanted to get into the computer market in a much bigger way—vertically integrated from the basic desktop all the way to the big mainframes.

We soon encountered the challenges of that fast-moving market. Not only was the inventory expensive, but the models were changing before we could sell them. This was a very low-margin business, and each Computer Shoppe required as much corporate overhead as our other stores with ten times the revenues.

We did eventually open seven stores, hanging on to the business through the 1980s, but we concluded that we had chosen a bad time to get into the business since the technology at the consumer level was still in its early days. We did all right business-to-business. As a storefront operation for consumers, however, we found that any profit was too low, and the risk was far too high. In 1989, we shut the stores down.

Mr. HOW

In 1983, we purchased a company in southern Florida that sold construction and home-improvement products. The store was called Home-Owners Warehouse, which we renamed Mr. HOW and began expanding into several markets.

For several years I'd resisted getting involved in the home-improvement space. In 1979, I rejected a suggestion that I meet with a couple of fellows in Atlanta who were opening hardware stores and looking to raise money. "No way," I said. "I don't want to be in the hardware business." Later that year, when we opened our first four Service Merchandise stores in Florida, that chain from Atlanta moved in right next to us. Our new neighbor was called Home Depot, and it was looking for another round of money. I still wasn't interested. "Nope," I said. "We're sticking with what we know."

One day in 1983, a friend called me. "Take a look in the *Wall Street Journal* at how Home Depot is doing," he said.

I checked the listings and sighed. "I really missed it, didn't I?"

"Well, I've got a friend starting a hardware store like theirs in Miami," he told me. I made a beeline down to Florida to check it out. The owner had knocked off the Home Depot concept, almost to a T, and was looking to open others. I told him to let me know if he was interested in selling his operation. A week after the store opened, we struck a deal.

While considering the purchase, I learned that a startup wholesale club in Seattle was looking for investors. I flew there to check it out—and I didn't like the vibe. The place was in disarray, and the CEO was dressed in a tweed sport coat with elbow patches and seemed just too good looking to take seriously. He introduced us to the company president, a big, sweaty fellow in a white shirt and tie. *These guys are going to take our money and run,* I thought.

I couldn't have been more mistaken. Both men turned out to be rising stars in the industry. They were a great team on their way to big success. They called their little venture Costco, and the retail industry later would name the CEO as the retailer of the century.

Should we invest? Despite my first impressions, I still saw an opportunity there. I met with the Service Merchandise management to discuss the matter. We could acquire a 25 percent stake in Costco for $15 million or all of Mr. HOW for that price. I was inclined to do both, but the consensus was to do the latter. We turned down a deal that today probably would be worth $50 billion.

As we were closing in on the deal, the owner gave my father and me a personal tour of the store. He stopped to show us a self-service kiosk where customers could plan projects. "We call this Mr. HOW," he said. "If you want to build a deck, you can put in the dimensions and get a printout of everything you need to build it, and Mr. HOW will tell you where to find the materials in

We turned down a deal that today probably would be worth $50 billion.

our store." The kiosk reminded me of our own Silent Sam system that we were rolling out.

I was impressed; Daddy was not. "I guarantee you," he said, "that if we make this deal and I could put a jewelry department in here, we'd make a lot more money than your Mr. HOW could ever bring in."

Within two years, we had twenty-seven Mr. HOW stores in various markets, including five in the Chicago area. However, we lost our top manager, the original owner who had stayed on to run our stores. He became frustrated with the pace of construction and resigned. He took with him a wealth of experience and insights. A year later, he founded Office Depot.

Meanwhile, we had the opportunity to focus on a couple of long-sought acquisitions that were in line with our core business, the catalog showrooms. We soon realized that the hardware business would be a drain on our operations. We lacked the infrastructure to do it all. Mr. HOW had to go. Once we decided that, there was no point in searching for the best managers who could have steered those stores to success. Instead, we found a buyer and could have sold the chain for a profit, but the deal fell through. We ended up selling the stores piecemeal.

Zimm's Jewelers

My father retired because my mother needed dialysis and they wanted to move to Florida, where the clinics were far better than in Nashville. "You guys love Florida," I told them. "So why don't you go there and take care of Mother, and y'all live the good life." They had bought an apartment in Miami, so it was a natural step—although Daddy had no intention of slowing down.

We set up a home computer for him, which gave him access to the inner workings of Service Merchandise. In those days, the network connections all were dial up. Whenever I would try to call the apartment, the line was busy. All day long, he was sitting there examining what every buyer was doing, particularly the jewelry selections.

I could track his movements like clockwork, though. I knew that he took Mother for dialysis on Monday, Wednesday, and Friday mornings, and after dropping her off, he would head right over to the nearby Service Merchandise store, which was in a mall about twenty minutes from the clinic. And about half an hour after that, almost to the minute, I knew that I would be answering my phone.

"Good morning, Daddy. How's Mother? And what do you want to tell me is wrong today?" It was always the same. The store didn't have enough inventory, or it didn't have enough help—some variation on one of those themes.

For my own sanity, I needed to stop those calls, so one day I issued an executive order at a staff meeting. "The next time I hear from my father that our Miami store on 163rd Street is out of anything or doesn't have enough help, you're all fired!" Everyone laughed. "From now on," I said, "there's no budget for that store. Do whatever you want." The store had been doing about $8 million in revenue. The next year, it topped $12 million.

One day in the spring of 1985, I stopped by to visit my parents. As we sat chatting in the den, Mother turned to Daddy and said, "Show him your shoebox." He pulled a box from the cabinet under the TV and handed it to me. Inside were twenty or thirty pieces of jewelry with tags on them, ready to sell. I picked up a necklace and dangled it from a finger.

"Show him your closet," Mother said next. He opened the door to a long walk-in closet and flicked on the light. The shelves were lined with shoeboxes. I opened one after another, and each was filled with tagged jewelry.

"I'm going to open a jewelry store," Daddy explained. "I'm going to call it Zimm's," he said. "Zimm's Jewelers."

Daddy arranged to open a Zimm's in Nashville. "I'm going to show y'all how to run a store," he said. Soon he was boasting a million dollars in sales, which was a lot of business for a small jewelry store. Then he opened a second store and pulled in a million and a half.

And then he passed away.

Daddy was in his element during that final year of his life, until we lost him after heart surgery. He was basking in the jewelry business that he had come to love. I respected his initiative and applauded his success. Without him, though, I saw no need for those two Zimm's stores that duplicated what we sold at Service.

When I made that announcement, however, there was rebellion in the ranks of our senior jewelry people: "Those stores were Mr. Harry's baby! Don't close them! Open more to honor him!" Such was the affection for my father throughout the ranks, and though I admired their loyalty, I didn't share their enthusiasm. I agreed to open one more Zimm's, but I didn't go out of my way to make it a success. In fact, I chose such a poor site for that store that it was bound to fail. Jewelry already was our focus in our showrooms across the nation. We didn't need another distraction. We had plenty of other concerns competing for our attention.

The Lingerie Store

One of those distractions had been a brief entry into the lingerie business. During a visit to my parents, Arlene and I stopped to eat at a deli, and she visited a lingerie store in the same shopping center. "I think it would be fun to open a store like that," she told me.

I had our accountants work up a business plan, and the prospects looked good. So we started with two stores and grew to four—with two in Nashville, one in Knoxville, and one in Ann Arbor, Michigan.

That experiment didn't last long. We didn't get the right managers in place to operate those stores, and it took us only a year or two to conclude that we had better things to do than present ourselves as a discount version of Victoria's Secret.

SWEET REVENGE

If everything doesn't go your way in a deal, just wait—
and if you stay in the business long enough, you'll get

your chance. A particularly soul-satisfying example of that principle came my way one day in 1984 as I was closing a deal to buy four stores, in Maryland and Delaware. The owner was getting out of the catalog showroom business, and these were his last stores to sell.

A dozen years earlier, this same fellow had sold us a discount store that he operated in Huntsville, Alabama, before entering the catalog business. A week later, I got a call from my construction foreman who went to the store to begin the remodel. "They took the air conditioners," he said. I was on the phone in a flash with the seller.

"Well, we needed them in our new store," he explained. "And I figured they weren't part of the building." I begged to differ, but there wasn't much I could do at that point.

Come 1984, though, there was plenty I could do. At the settlement table, I handed him the check for the purchase. He and his lawyers checked the figures— and noticed it was short of what we agreed. When they asked what was up, I handed over another piece of paper—a bill for the value of the air conditioners, plus twelve years of interest.

"You can't do that!" the owner protested. I suggested that he either pick up the bill or I'd hand back the keys to the building. The air turned a bit blue as he

contemplated the situation, but he relented—and I
got my sweet revenge.

Wilson and Ellman's Acquisitions

During our Mr. HOW expansion frenzy in 1985, we acquired the H.
J. Wilson and Ellman's chains. Ellman's was a clipboard operation, like
Service Merchandise, and had thirteen showrooms in Georgia and
North Carolina. Wilson's was one of the largest of the catalog opera-
tions, with eighty showrooms in twelve states, but it was self-service.
All those stores would need to be remodeled.

The Wilson's negotiations took three months. While I was in
New York to finally sign that deal, I got a call to come to Atlanta if I
wanted to buy Ellman's. We signed with Wilson's on a Friday night,
then flew to Atlanta—and after three hours of negotiations, we signed
with Ellman's on Saturday afternoon. On Monday morning, about
the time of the opening bell on Wall Street, we announced both deals.

Though it might have seemed to some that we had gone crazy,
these both were long-sought transactions finally coming to fruition.
I also knew that we didn't have enough money to be doing all these
ventures at the same time—Mr. HOW, Wilson's, and Ellman's.

Ellman's was an easy transition because of the similarity of our
clipboard operations. It was the eighty Wilson's stores that were the
challenge, and our first big problem was that we immediately took
down the Wilson's signs on the storefronts and then couldn't get
permits to put up our Service Merchandise signs. We went through
that Christmas with no signs on the buildings. Not good. And then
we discovered that a lot of the Wilson's inventory just wasn't compat-

ible with ours, including their apparel line that we tried for a while to continue. We were confusing our customers.

The attention that we were devoting to Wilson's and Ellman's was further delaying construction of the Mr. HOW stores. They were not our priority. Meanwhile, we still were building Service Merchandise showrooms—thirteen that year alone—and acquiring other stores, including locations in Gainesville and Leesburg, Florida. Something had to give. It was clear that Mr. HOW would be history.

And it became clear we would be in a financial pinch that year. We hadn't been able to complete a profitable deal on selling Mr. HOW. The Wilson's inventory issue and the costs of remodeling those eighty stores were costing us dearly. We realized that we would show a loss and wrote off everything we could, trying to clean up our balance sheet.

The Power of Relationships

In 1986, after years of strong profits, the company took a loss, the only one we ever had experienced. On sales of over $2.5 billion, we lost $47 million. We weren't alone in our financial challenges. Best Products also posted a loss that year, and some catalog showroom operators were going out of business. Determined to continue delivering the quality, service, and value that our customers had come to expect—without them, we would be nothing—we kept our focus on our core of jewelry, gifts, and home decor. We remained ever attentive to technology, devising more efficient ways to assess trends, track inventory, and improve distribution.

In the midst of our financial problems, I got a call from the head of the Credit Managers Association. Would I come to Oklahoma City for their annual meeting and tell the group just what we planned to do? I agreed, and he scheduled me to talk at 6:00 a.m. "No problem," I said. "I'll be there."

When I got to the hotel about midnight to check in, the night clerk picked up the phone, tapped a few buttons, and said, "He's here." It seems the group's chairman had been calling him every half hour to see whether I'd shown up.

The next morning, I walked into a room meant for twenty people that was packed with about fifty—standing room only—eager to hear what I might have to say. My heart was in my throat, but I explained how we planned to get through this difficult stretch.

"The reason we aren't paying you," I said, "is because we don't know what we owe you, and we don't have the money—but if anybody here is really hurting badly and we're causing your business to suffer, just call me. We'll get a payment to you right away." I thanked the group and turned to leave. I heard somebody start clapping, and then the whole room joined in. I got a standing ovation.

> "But if anybody here is really hurting badly and we're causing your business to suffer, just call me."

Our relationship with our vendors was crucial. It was their cooperation that had enabled us to grow our business and also get through those troubled times. Treat people right, my parents had taught me, and they will be there for you. A few of the smaller vendors took me up on my offer, and I'm proud to say that we made sure that our problems didn't hurt them. We learned from this experience.

We had a great thing going for us in our Service Merchandise stores, and we soon recovered, listing on the New York Stock

Exchange. We got rid of what was distracting us. I am forever grateful to the many vendors who extended us credit. Our relationships, as much as anything, helped us to recover. One of those relationships, for example, would bring us an entire shipping container of Barbie dolls, fifty thousand strong, just before Christmas of 1990—and our computer system distributed them so efficiently that we sold them all in four days.

I recalled my father's words to me when I was a little boy holding his hand at the New York Toy Fair: "Get to know people and make friends, Raymond. They'll trust you and take care of you."

"Could You Lend Me Ten Dollars?"

One of the ways that we were operating smarter was an automated warehouse of 752,000 square feet that we opened in 1986 in Montgomery, New York, to serve our numerous stores in the Northeast. In the early days of Walmart, Sam Walton opened a similar automated warehouse, and though he was a big fan of efficiency, you wouldn't have known it from his initial reaction.

Sam invited me once to one of his Saturday morning managers meetings in which they would review the good and the bad of the week. Sam scowled as he peered at a computer printout. "What's with *this*? We invest all this money in that new warehouse, and here I find out our payroll is 2 percent higher than it was when we kept all our stuff in the old barn out back." He looked at his managers. "You've got ten days to reduce that payroll, or we're shutting her down."

Sam wasn't serious, of course. He was just demanding an effective operation. He was a great guy with an amazing mind who soaked up information like a sponge. We sometimes had breakfast together when he visited Nashville. One day at the grand opening in Nashville of one of the first Sam's Club stores, he shook my hand warmly, then held on to it as he escorted me to a TV crew that was filming a spot on the event. "I want you all to meet Raymond Zimmerman," he said as the camera rolled. "He's the CEO of Service Merchandise in town, but from now on, it's right here that everyone's going to be buying their merchandise. Right, Raymond?"

I laughed and turned to the cameraman. "If that goes on the air, I'll never run another ad on your station again!"

When he invited me to that staff meeting, Sam also insisted that I stay overnight at his house. I needed to go to Fayetteville early the next day to check out a site where we wanted to build a store, and he offered to drive me there. "You would be building it in a lot right next door to us," he said, "and I know the fellow who owns that dirt. We'll tell him we want you there."

We didn't really consider each other to be competitors, other than the fact that any merchant, even the corner drugstore, was going for the same retail dollar. Sam mostly had been focusing on small towns, and our company favored city locations. Service Merchandise and Walmart appealed to different types of consumers. Sam wasn't focusing on jewelry and upscale gifts. We weren't worried, at the time, about hurting each other.

The next morning at six o'clock, as we bumped along a two-lane road in Arkansas, the car's engine sputtered and quit. We were out of gas. We had just crested a hill, and down the road I could see a filling station. We coasted to the pump just as the owner was coming out to unlock it for the day.

"We ought to go to Vegas, with this kind of luck," Sam said as he stepped out of the car to fill the tank. A few minutes later, he looked at me sheepishly through the open window. "Raymond, I need a favor," the world's richest man said. "Could you lend me ten dollars?"

As I peeled a sawbuck from my wallet, I smiled. Here were two men of business, each leading a major enterprise, engaging in a simple exchange based wholly on trust. He had helped me, and I was helping him—and I don't know a better way to do business than that.

Years later, I told that story to Sam's son, Rob, during a cab ride to an investors conference in New York. "I can't say, as I recall, whether your dad ever got around to paying me back," I told him.

"Really? Well, I'll take care of that right now!" he said, offering me a ten.

"Ha! Ten dollars? There's interest on top of that, don't forget," I told him, trying to keep a straight face. "And you know, I just love telling this story about your daddy—but, hey, for a million dollars, I'll stop!"

A Bid for Best

By 1988, Service Merchandise was experiencing a healthy recovery. Our sales that year edged above $3 billion dollars. The market at the time was weak, with our stock trading at six dollars a share, and we were approached by a venture capital firm that wanted to take us private again in a leveraged buyout.

We eventually agreed on a price, and we took out a billion-dollar line of credit for the deal, expecting to use half of it to buy back the stock (at ten dollars a share for fifty million shares outstanding) and the other half as working capital. Before we could pen the deal, though, our stock more than doubled in price. To buy back all the stock at that point would have severely overleveraged us, so it made no sense to continue.

We began to look for other ways to use the credit line to further expand our company. One of those ways would be to acquire Best Products, giving us unrivaled supremacy in the catalog showroom industry. In a merger, we also would effectively acquire Modern Merchandising, for which Best Products had outbid us back in '82. We saw our opportunity when another venture capital firm approached Best Products seeking to buy the company. We jumped in with our own offer—but we were outbid.

That billion-dollar line of credit ended up having three lives. After a leveraged buyout and our bid for Best Products didn't happen, the company decided how it ultimately would make use of that money. The board announced a recapitalization plan that included a dividend to shareholders of ten dollars a share, or $500 million.

Right before the announcement, I got a call from the same gentleman who had summoned me to the credit managers meeting a few years earlier. He invited me to come to their Nashville meeting to give a talk. "This recap we're doing is quite a big deal," I told him. "Everyone's going to want to know all about it. Better reserve a big room." He did. Seven people showed up, most of them my Service Merchandise colleagues. I guess good news isn't particularly interesting. It was clear to all that our company was doing just fine.

True to a Vision

I often think of that long-gone day when Daddy showed me his shoeboxes. Whatever else we might try on for size, jewelry was the heart of our enterprise. We once had an opportunity to open a Service Merchandise store on Fifty-Seventh Street in Manhattan, which I had long wanted to do. When I went up to sign the lease, though, the building's owner had some misgivings. "We love your catalog. It's fabulous," he said. "But we can't have you competing with all the jewelry retailers over on Forty-Seventh Street. We're excited to bring you here, but we don't want your jewelry." Clear enough. And I didn't want that deal.

What that gentleman didn't understand was that we weren't in the appliance business or the electronics business or the toy business. We were in the jewelry business primarily, and it was my father's passion for it that gave Service Merchandise that focus. He and I each had our strengths, but neither of us knew how to run a store. We had hundreds of them, coast to coast, but we didn't run them. We managed them. We hired the people who ran them, and when we made good choices, it worked out. We learned during our years of booming growth that running a business is all about those people.

Success comes from staying true to a vision. Throughout my years at Service Merchandise, our people constantly came to me with what they believed were great initiatives that we should pursue. I had what I called the fifteen-minute rule: tell me about your idea for five minutes, and I'll respond for five minutes, and we'll talk it over for five minutes. And then I get to make the decision.

I understood the value of fresh ideas, but innovation must be strategic. A lot of those folks could say precisely *how* we should change the way we did things, but I wanted to make sure they could express *why* we should change. Our success led us to experiment in the 1980s with a few ideas that weren't compatible with our business model. We learned that even as a company prospers and branches out, it must remain faithful to its roots. That's what builds customer loyalty—and that's a truly precious commodity.

It's the 1990s ...

- The US launches Operation Desert Storm in Iraq.

- The Soviet Union dissolves.

- Princess Diana dies in a tunnel crash.

- President Bill Clinton is impeached.

- The euro makes its debut.

    ... and Service Merchandise reaches its retail peak.

Through the Years ...

- 1992: Service Merchandise earns $84 million, its highest ever.

- 1993: The company begins "ville strategy" of smaller stores away from cities.

- 1995: Raymond Zimmerman marries Etta Gross-Edelstein.

- 1995: The company reaches its peak of 409 stores.

- 1997: Raymond steps down as chairman.

CHAPTER 6

Turning the Page, 1990–2000

IT WAS THREE O'CLOCK on Christmas morning, and the caller from Kansas obviously had been drinking. "Hey, I'm putting together my kid's hobbyhorse here, and it's missing one of the springs."

"Oh, no. What would you like me to do?" I asked.

"Well, since we're both up, how about you bring me one?"

"All right," I said. "On my way." There's not much else to say to a somewhat pickled parent struggling to assemble a toy in the wee hours. The next day, I had our shipping department open a box in the warehouse, take out a spring, and send it to him—but I felt bad that a little one's toy wasn't working on Christmas morning.

I never had an unlisted number. I wanted to be accessible to any customer any time. Every catalog had my picture inside the cover with a message to our customers. My administrative assistants knew that the rule was to put all calls through to me from anyone asking for me by name. I talked to everybody, and I loved getting those calls—though at times I wondered why they figured the CEO of Service Merchandise would be the best guy to reach. But if they thought so, why shouldn't I?

I heard everything: "I lost the box for the engagement ring I bought from you, and I'm supposed to pop the question tonight!" or "Your store sold the last Barbie an hour ago. What am I supposed to do now?" Every second of those calls was worth it. We tried to abide by the adage that the customer is always right. Once, we provided a thirty-dollar doll to a shopper for ten bucks because the cheaper doll was sold out. She was delighted. How many times do you suppose she told family and friends about the great deal she got from the fine folks down at Service Merchandise?

I recall answering the phone in my home one evening to hear the voice of an angry woman. "You sold me this fancy iron for $28.98, but you changed the settings! And now I've scorched my husband's shirt. So are you gonna pay for it?"

"Well, uh …" I was groping for the right words to calm her down when I heard a hoot of laughter from the next room. My wife Etta, whom I married in 1995, had made the call, disguising her voice. She pulled that kind of stunt over and over. She got a kick out of seeing how tolerant I could be.

I had met Etta at a shopping center convention in Dallas. A real estate broker, she approached my colleagues and me to talk about some stores that we were closing. Later we met again in Atlanta, where she was the broker for a lease deal to open a baby store. I got that lease—and as it turned out, I got Etta too.

My marriage to Etta came with the added blessing of her little girl, Leya, who was five years old at the time. I had the privilege of participating in raising her—and the exquisite honor of formally becoming her adoptive daddy upon her twenty-first birthday.

As a child, Leya delighted in accompanying me on inspection visits to stores. We even gave her a company name tag as a junior associate. She was remarkably observant too. Leya would scope out the territory with me, and she told us that she could tell by my body language in the first ten steps into a store whether I was giving a thumbs up or a thumbs down to what I was seeing. I know there were times when the three of us were heading out to dinner or a movie and didn't get there because we made a "brief" stop at one of our stores. I should have resisted the temptation, but Leya, sweet kid, seemed just as happy with a McDonald's feast.

Etta became an avid watchdog of our store operations, insisting that we settle for nothing less than excellence and that every associate at every level contribute to building the company. I recall her coming home and nudging me awake one day as I was taking a nap. She was sobbing.

"I did a terrible thing," she said.

"You mean waking me up, right?"

"No, no." Etta was clutching a framed photograph of my parents—the photo that we displayed in all our stores. She explained that she had paid a visit to one of our stores and was deeply disturbed by what struck her as a disregard for excellence. "Raymond, I was just so annoyed. The place was a mess—and, well, I went over the counter and took their picture down," she said. "I told the manager it was a damned good thing they were already dead because if they'd seen that store, it would have killed them." She sighed. "And then I realized what I'd done." Her tears flowed again.

Those are but a few snapshots of life in the 1990s, the final decade in the Service Merchandise story. Business was flowing along well as the decade commenced, despite the steep recession of the first year or two. We reached record earnings in 1992 and 1993, and our revenues kept growing, from $3.4 billion in sales in 1990 to more than $4 billion by mid-decade. In 1990, we introduced a national gift registry that customers could access in all our stores. It would instantly update throughout our chain whenever items on the registry were purchased. In 1992, we opened a store in the Mall of America, the world's largest shopping complex. By 1995, we had reached a peak of 409 stores, 75 more than we had as the decade began.

"WHAT'S THE CODE?"

We never were big on the traditional analytics at Service Merchandise. Our real estate department consisted of only three people. We didn't need to put a lot of brainpower into figuring out what would be a good fit for us. We did it more by the gut. It's always wise to know your figures and to size up the competition, of course, but there's also much to be said for swift and decisive action when forging a deal.

That's what builds relationships, and that's how we got the first shot at a lot of great locations. We acted as partners. Shopping center developers are happy when they have a financeable lease in hand, and we aimed to deliver. We weren't necessarily their first choice, because only during certain times of year did we bring in a lot of traffic to the shopping center. Still, we could give them a long-term financeable lease, a good-looking store, and a quick answer that didn't analyze the deal to death. When you do right by people, they do right by you. Respect breeds respect.

When it came to sizing up our competition, respect goes a long way, but so does due diligence. We did our share of sleuthing to see what other stores were up to. We knew that places like Costco and Sam's Club, for example, took a flat margin markup on their merchandise. All we had to do was deduct the margin to see what those stores were paying—and whether we were being overcharged for the same items, which was sometimes the case.

So we kept our eyes and ears open. Often as I walked through a store, an associate or manager would greet me with "Can I help you?"

I would launch into small talk and eventually get around to asking, just out of curiosity, "So how much business has this store been doing, anyway?" And eight out of ten times, they would tell me. We got all kinds of sales figures that way.

One year during the holiday season, I got the bright idea of calling our competitors' stores right after closing time. They would still answer the phone sometimes, and I'd ask for the cash office. "Hi, I'm from the home office," I would say. "How'd we do today?" Most of the time, they would tell me the sales.

"Easy as can be," I told our people—and then it occurred to me that I probably wasn't the only one out there thinking themselves clever. I issued a warning that nobody was to be giving out our sales figures to just anyone.

One evening, after the grand opening of a new store in Cambridge, Massachusetts, I was telling Daddy that business had been brisk. "Well, what were the numbers?" he asked. I told him I would find out. I dialed the store and asked for the manager, whom I knew well, and told him that I had heard the store was jam packed all day.

"Yup," he said.

"So how much did you bring in?"

"What's the code?" he asked me.

"Code? I don't need any code! How much were your sales today?"

"Let me ask *you* something," he said. "Which do you suppose would look better on my resume—that I got fired because I told you or because I didn't tell you?"

The manager wouldn't budge, so I placed a call to our vice president of stores. "Okay, okay. What have you guys done, put out a gag order? Tell me the freaking code!"

The VP burst out laughing. "How can I be sure you're who you say you are?" he asked. Finally, he relented: "The code is 'One Billion'—that was our company-wide target for revenue."

I called the manager again. "I've got two words for you," I said. "One billion."

"All righty then!" he said, chuckling. "$162,000."

The "Ville" Strategy

In the 1990s, we took steps to expand our long-standing practice of positioning stores closer to the people. To fully explain, bear with me as I go back two decades to a day when I took an exit off Interstate 24 in Tennessee.

I was driving from Nashville to Chattanooga to attend a shopping center convention and pulled off to get gas in what seemed like a little town in the middle of nowhere. But I had trouble getting to the station because traffic was lined up. When I finally made my way through the jam, I asked the gas station attendant what was going on.

"Oh, it's just this new shopping center that's opened up here," he said, pointing down the road to a building that was the focus of all the attention. "They brought in one of those new Walmarts." At the time, Sam Walton's spotlight was on small towns and villages with maybe five thousand or ten thousand people. I went into the store to check out the scene. It was ten o'clock at night, and the place was packed.

For the next couple decades, I remembered that image of all those cars pouring

Not everyone loves a long drive to a mall ... we need to do more to get closer to the people.

into a rural parking lot. *Not everyone loves a long drive to a mall,* I thought. *Maybe we need to do more to get closer to the people.* We mostly had located in major metropolitan areas, which meant a store in one city pulled customers from a region about halfway to the next city where we had a store.

That's why I declined an offer in 1993 to put a Service Merchandise in Clarksville, Tennessee. "No, you're just too close to our Rivergate store in north Nashville," I told the mall developer, who was a friend of mine. Clarksville was only fifty miles northwest of Nashville. "We draw $3 million worth of business from the Clarksville area already," I said.

"Why don't you come on up anyway?" my friend asked. "Just take a look around." We met the next Sunday and walked through the mall, which was a pretty typical one. Best part of the trip was just getting to spend some time together. As I was leaving, though, I looked across the street and saw something else that had become pretty typical. A shopping center had opened there with a Walmart as the center attraction. I drove around back of the store. The way you used to tell how much business a Walmart was doing was to see how many storage trailers were behind it. In those days, before the supercenters, the average store had six or eight of them. This store had forty-five storage trailers out back.

Nothing else had opened in that shopping center. The developer was looking for tenants. I asked my real estate people the next day to go up and see if they could make a deal. "Go scope it out, and see what you come up with," I said. They saw a conflict right away. What would a Clarksville store do to our sales at Rivergate? "I'm thinking something smaller," I explained. "There's a lot of business up there, and we should test the waters."

"Well, if you're going to be thinking that way," one of the crew suggested, "why not Cookeville?" Cookeville was about halfway between Nashville and Knoxville, about a hundred miles from each. We had two stores in Knoxville and a dozen or so in the Carolinas, which meant our trucks were passing through Cookeville on Interstate 40 several times a night. I sent him on a scouting mission there, and he called to report that the only space he could find immediately available was a 1,500-square-foot store at a small mall. "Make a deal," I said, to his astonishment.

It was a little bitty space by our standards—our full-size stores were more than thirty times as large, at fifty thousand square feet— but I felt confident that we could figure out a good use. I started thinking about the business model of a company called Argos in England. The CEO of Argos once had taken me on a tour of one of his stores. He showed me a drop-off area where the lorry drivers left merchandise overnight to be stocked the next morning. I figured that in our little space in Cookeville, we could put four Silent Sam kiosks where customers could purchase orders that would print out in Nashville. We then could have our truckers, who were passing through Cookeville anyway, drop off the merchandise overnight, just like at Argos. It would be there for the customers in the morning.

And so we ran that experiment. That little store with no inventory did a million dollars in business that year, even though it didn't have a jewelry display. One day the manager called to report that, in the same mall, a seven-thousand-square-foot store was available. "Grab it," I said. The store still was relatively tiny but big enough to squeeze in a jewelry counter, as well as to display a few items from each of our other departments. It was a limited selection, but shoppers always could order from the catalog too. That store rang up $3.5 million in sales in its first year. We came to see that the Cookeville trade area was far larger than we had realized, serving a couple hundred thousand people.

This was the beginning of what we would call our "ville strategy," because we started out establishing those small stores in towns with that suffix. One of our first, for example, was in a new mall in Douglasville, not far from Atlanta. We set up a distribution center at the former Ellman's corporate office in Atlanta, where the orders would print out for goods to be loaded onto the delivery trucks.

Demographically, our stores were always changing, and we needed to be alert to that. Now and then, an area would deteriorate to the point where a standard-size store would need to close or move to a better area a few miles away, at significant expense. The ville strategy would give us more flexibility, and it was central to a strategy that I envisioned for the 1990s.

Those small stores were highly profitable: the rent was low because of their size, we didn't have a lot of overhead, and we didn't need many personnel. I anticipated opening a lot of them, coast to coast, each with a complete jewelry department along with a sampling of merchandise. As I saw it, they would introduce Service Merchandise to many thousands of customers who otherwise might never have known us at all. By getting closer to the customer, I saw how we could generate a boatload of new business.

OFF TO THE RACES

In the summer of 1993, Service Merchandise had the honor of sponsoring the Indianapolis 500 entry of Willy T. Ribbs, who had been the first African American to compete in the race.

Also backing Ribbs that year was Bill Cosby, so we worked out an arrangement: we would sponsor the race car with the comedian, and in return he would appear for four days in broadcast and print advertisements for our company.

The deal was for $3 million, with an option for a second year. And though I was rooting for Ribbs to win the race, I quipped that I hoped the car wasn't so fast that folks couldn't read *Service Merchandise* on its side.

Onward to Online

Early in the '90s, we recognized the potential of the internet and began looking for opportunities to make the most of it. Our catalog model required us to find efficient ways to get rid of discontinued inventory that had been dropped from the latest printing. We marked it down in the stores, but, by my calculations, we lost one sale of a full-price item for every two items we sold at discount. I would have liked a magic wand that would make discontinued inventory vanish. I approached the home shopping channels about featuring those items, but they weren't interested. They had been stung by companies that failed to ship and fulfill the viewers' orders.

So what next? The internet had been bursting onto the scene. Could that be the magic wand? I asked our merchandising internet people to pick out thirty or so odds and ends of electronics and cameras that weren't selling.

"What are you going to do with them?" they asked.

I NEVER WORKED A DAY IN MY LIFE

"I'm going to put them on a website."

"What's that?"

"I'm not really sure that I know," I said, "but I know you guys are going to figure it out."

My plan was to put up those thirty items online at a bargain price and then take 25 percent more off one of the items each day until they were gone. We would be building an internet presence while disposing of the discontinued stuff. Didn't work. We sold none of it. It seemed that nobody felt confident in supplying their credit card information online.

This was before the digital revolution would begin challenging brick-and-mortar operations a decade or so later. Internet shopping wasn't a phenomenon then, so our "ville strategy" was an attractive opportunity within easy driving distance. In those days, people mostly visited stores, not websites. Far from ignoring the internet, however, we embraced it early. In 1996, we launched our online presence with a website offering a seven-thousand-item catalog.

Imagine how it would play out today, well into the internet age, if we had gone on to establish thousands of those ville outlets around the country. With that infrastructure in place, I can imagine multitudes of online shoppers placing orders for pickup at those stores or for home delivery from our network of distribution hubs. We would be doing what Amazon is doing today.

THE POWER OF THE GREETERS

Sam Walton told me years ago that one of the hardest systems he had ever set up was the door greeter program. When we tried it at Service Merchandise about 1990, I suggested scripting the interaction with customers. "Tell the greeters exactly what you expect them to say," I told those responsible for hiring and training them.

We tested our greeter program in Orlando, Florida, where we had six stores. A month after it started, I went down to see how it was working. I got a different reaction from the greeters at each store: some said hello, some said nothing, some even turned the other way. I put out the word that we should hire friendly people as greeters. "This might seem obvious," I said, "but let's make sure we give that job to people who like to be around people."

In 1992, we held the grand opening of a new store near our corporate headquarters in Tennessee, and we invited our vendors to celebrate with us. A few of the vendors asked if we might pay a visit to the operations at nearby Target and Kmart and Walmart stores to check out the competition, so I took them on a tour. At Target, the greeter just looked at us. At Kmart, the greeter walked away.

And then we entered Walmart. "Welcome to Walmart!" the greeter said brightly. "And aren't you all looking smart in those coats and ties!" She looked to be nearly ninety but with plenty of energy to fetch us a shopping cart.

We took a stroll through the store, and in the "power alley," a prime selling spot, we noticed a sale promotion of two bags of potatoes for ninety-nine cents. And then we noticed that every shopping cart in the store seemed to have two bags of potatoes in it. Was there even one cart without them? "There's one!" I said as we were leaving. And just then a shopper came hustling up to the cart and dropped in her two bags. I don't know if all those folks needed potatoes, but a deal is a deal.

Time to Step Aside

I loved the automatic air conditioner in my new Cadillac, except when the system didn't work, which was often—and that's not cool. After it failed for the third time, I demanded that the mechanic get the service manager on the line.

"Mr. Zimmerman," he said, "it's doing what it's supposed to do. You just don't understand how air conditioning works in the summertime."

"Listen here, young man," I began. And stopped. What had I just called him? *Young man?* It was 1993, and I had just turned sixty—and when those words came out of my mouth, I felt ancient.

GOODBYE TO THE BMW

One year in the early 1990s, we were one of Panasonic's biggest customers in the world, with $300 million in sales. The next year, we were down to $10 million. We apparently fell from the company's graces, for whatever reason, but it was reason enough for

Service Merchandise to focus more on where it was sourcing its products.

"From now on," I announced to a group of our company executives, "if you're driving a company car, it has to be an American brand." The executives were driving leased cars, so that could be easily accomplished. The car that I drove, however, was company owned—and it was a BMW. I was fond of it.

"So, *ahem*, Raymond, about that car you're driving," one or another of my people would remind me now and then. "You know—that *German* car you're driving?" They were good natured but went straight to the point. Our company was trying to do its part to reduce American dependence on foreign factories and protect American jobs, and I hadn't exactly been swift to follow my own edict. One must lead by example, and soon I was going about my business in a new Cadillac.

For more than three decades, I had been developing and growing Service Merchandise to new heights. Lately I had been hearing numerous suggestions from colleagues about how we needed to be doing things differently, such as opening the mall jewelry stores. I pooh-poohed the idea. All my career, I had been a champion for innovation, eager to try new concepts and technologies, and now I found myself blocking a lot of new ideas. In retrospect, I'm glad that I shortstopped many of the questionable suggestions that came my way. Still, a bad idea doesn't disprove the value of modernizing. I was adopting a mindset of *This is how we've always done things, and it's how we'll keep doing it*. Was I becoming rigid in my ways? *That's not good*, I thought.

One morning while shaving, I leaned close to the mirror and looked at the lines on my face. "Raymond," I said to my reflection, "you need to get out." I felt it was time that someone else take a turn at the wheel. We'd made $84 million in 1992, more earnings than ever before, and we made $82 million the following year. Still, I recognized the company would need to draw on an abundance of fresh ideas to keep up that pace in an increasingly complex retail marketplace. I had brought us a long way. We needed someone else for the next leg of the journey. The company would need to rethink the way it did business, and I knew that I should not be the one doing it.

Across the land, we faced stiff competition from the new breed of big-box retailers able to offer a wide selection of specialty merchandise at a deeper discount—Best Buy, Circuit City, and Bed Bath & Beyond, as a few examples. We had our sight and sound department, and we were proud of it. Best Buy, though, seemed to carry every audio and visual product out there. We were a great company with a dedicated workforce and countless loyal customers. We had attained retail dominance when those other guys were concepts waiting to be born. Now more than ever, though, we needed to brainstorm for our future.

And so began our search for my successor. I interviewed dozens of prospects, trying to weed out the know-it-all types from the let's-work-it-out types, and by 1995 we had a new CEO. I stayed on for a while as chairman, but it was hard to watch our numbers continuing to dwindle and the company closing stores. In my tenure, we had opened several of the "ville" stores. I had envisioned thousands of them around the country, but that was not to be.

A Birthday Farewell

The new leadership pursued a variety of initiatives as the new millennium approached. The company sought to upgrade the jewelry and home furnishing departments with more expensive product lines, at the same time cutting out underperforming categories such as toys and electronics—but in so doing, also reducing the foot traffic that generated a lot of those jewelry and home furnishing sales.

Some of the losses that the company saw in 1997 ($91 million) and 1998 ($110 million) resulted from a strategy of remodeling many of our full-size fifty-thousand-square-foot stores to half that size and leasing out the other half to other retailers—Office Depot, for example, or Staples, or whoever could use twenty-five thousand square feet. It was an attempt to bring in revenue from the rents, but remodeling is expensive and disrupts business, and you don't get that rent money from day one. Those expenses become write-offs that hurt the earnings—not to mention the write-offs from the dozens of stores that the company had been shuttering and from the liquidation of all that inventory.

The shopping experience in our stores also was changing. Instead of the familiar clipboards, customers now were collecting barcoded pull tags in the showroom to take to the cashiers. Many showrooms were converted to also accommodate the traditional way of shopping—and eventually all the stores gave up on the catalog-style approach for which Service Merchandise had long been known. They eventually discontinued the catalog itself.

On April 4, 1997, my sixty-fourth birthday, I announced to the board that I was leaving. I was ready to turn the page to my next chapter. Might I have turned around the company's fortunes if I had stayed on to reassume the leadership? Could I have done any better in this brave new world of retail? I do not know.

I do know this: the Service Merchandise family had a great run and a lot of fun for a good many years, and my mother and father can be eternally proud of what they created and accomplished. I am a man of eighty-nine years as I write these words, so I suppose in due course I'll get the chance to tell them all about it. And this above all: Not a single day ever felt like work to me. In Pulaski, and Nashville, from the East coast to the West, this company was my passion. I left while I still was in love.

> *This company was my passion. I left*
> *while I still was in love.*

The Hours We Shared:
Reflections on Our Time Together

Here are some of the special moments and lifelong memories that members of our Service Merchandise family have related to us as they look back on some of the best years of their lives. "I would do it all again," one of these writers tells us—and I must say that I wholeheartedly share that sentiment.—Raymond Zimmerman

CHRIS AND DAWN SCHWARTZ

My husband and I met working at SMC in Derby, Connecticut, when we were seventeen years old. We have been married now for thirty-two years and have three children. We had such great friends from that time, and I love seeing the different stories on Facebook of others who had the same experience while working there. There were several marriages that came out of that Unit 829 in Derby. Some met working together, and others met through friends who worked there. I can't even count the babies and grandbabies that came from that one store—but so many!

 ## KAREN M. GEIGER (SMITH)

Mr. Zimmerman was known for traveling around and visiting stores. He had never been to our store, and the group of us were dying to have him visit, especially since we had relocated and our new store was gorgeous. We were all so proud. We just knew that he would visit. We were all on a "Zimm alert"!

We had just made it through a fast-paced, successful Christmas season, and I was a little under the weather with bronchitis, so I was at home resting. Wouldn't you know it? Mr. Zimmerman stopped to visit the store! My girlfriends called me from the store to tell me that he was there. I was so excited—and mad that I wasn't going to get the chance to meet him.

Soooo, I told them to let me speak with him. At first, they said no, but I told them I was serious. I wanted to meet him so badly. So they paged him while I waited. He picked up the phone! I told him that I was so sorry that I was missing his visit but I was under the weather.

He said, "I am so sorry to hear that you are not feeling well. Thank you for all of your hard work. Give me your address. I will come visit you." I pretty near passed out! I thought to myself, *Now what are you going to do? You ran your mouth, and now he is coming to your apartment!* I rushed around screeching and scaring my cat, trying to clean up and straighten the apartment. Now, mind you, I was sick and looked a hot mess. The best I could muster was sweatpants and a sweatshirt. I kept running to the door to see if he was there yet.

He drove to my apartment with his wife and came in to say hi. He thanked me again and wished me better health. He hugged me goodbye. I had nothing to give but wanted to thank him—so me being a huge Garfield fan, I gave him some Garfield stickers that I had collected. Then he left ♥.

I was about twenty-four or twenty-five at the time, and it was the most amazing experience! I guess you could say that Mr. Zimmerman set the standard for me about what to expect from my leaders, how they should care and treat everyone—*everyone*! He was ahead of his time regarding emotional intelligence and soft skills.

I proudly worked for Service Merchandise for ten years, eventually becoming a jewelry manager. I worked in Salisbury, Maryland, and in Harrisburg and Lancaster, Pennsylvania, for Service Merchandise. I currently reside in New York, but I formed friendships that have stood the test of time. Anne, Michelle, and Matt—we are all still connected, all because of Service Merchandise. I had the very best of times working there.

 ## MARK WESTERMAN

I worked for Everett Purdy in Merchandise Systems back in 1982–1985—was known as his "Pen Pal." I left and had my own business in Florida for seven years, then decided to sell the business. I called Raymond for a reference. He could not remember my name, but Frank, who was in Raymond's office, said, "Raymond, you know him—it's Batman!"

At which time Raymond told me, "No, Batman, I'm not going to give you a reference—but I *will* give you a job! Can you be up here next Monday if I send you an airline ticket to headquarters? We have broken all the systems you worked on, and we need you to come up here and pave the dirt roads we built."

I accepted the job … and I worked in IT, where they thought I was a plant by Raymond! Of course, I rode that horse as long as I could, as I tried to get Kids Central off the ground with merchandise and financial systems patterned for fashion, fads, and staples.

 ## DANIEL KASPRZYCKI

In 1983 I applied for seasonal help at my local store here on Chicago's southeast side, SMC 130. After a year in the warehouse, I was promoted to receiving clerk. I liked this position and took this very seriously, checking in merchandise to our store. It was a lot of responsibility. I had been offered a warehouse supervisor job at a new store, about a half hour away, but refused it as I was going to be leaving the company to go into data processing.

In 1988 I left SMC after five years of working with some awesome people. I still shopped at SMC 130, as it was five minutes from my house. I was sad when the company closed their stores. About a year ago, I was able to reach Mr. Zimmerman by email after finding out about the SMC online store. I asked if, by chance, any old catalogs were still around, because I really wanted one. About a month later, I opened up a big envelope to find an old SMC spring and summer catalog from the early '80s, and it was autographed by Mr. Zimmerman himself. It brought back so many memories. SMC will always be a big part of my life—the people, the lifelong friendships, my first real job. Thank you, Zimmerman family!

LAURA WALTHER LANE

There are so many great memories that I don't even know where to begin. One of my greatest honors of my career was launching the gift registry for SMC. It was such a blast doing something that no company had ever done at the time. Working with the various teams to launch this endeavor was so much fun.

I remember Gayle (his secretary) and I visited his office many times. I was always so scared. I remember all of the memorial dinners, assisting with the tennis events, putting together the journal, and working to get the talent there, such as Sammy Davis Jr. I was also proud that Service Merchandise helped sponsor the first African American driver in the Indy 500. It was Willie T. Ribbs.

 DAN DEANS

I was the jewelry manager of the West Palm Beach store and noticed a man walking alone through our home accessories section. He had glasses on the top of his head. It's Mr. Zimmerman! I left my department and greeted him.

Me: "Hi, Mr. Zimmerman! Welcome to our store."

Raymond: "How are you?"

Me: "I'm great! Our jewelry department is leading the district in sales!"

Raymond: "Okay. Why?"

Me: "We've got our own goal-setting here, and it's working great."

Raymond: "Send it to my office this week."

Me: "Yes, sir, Mr. Zimmerman."

I made it into a report and sent it to Raymond, and he read it! Later, when I was a jewelry supervisor, the VP of jewelry called me up and asked why I went around him to give my report directly to Raymond. I answered that it happened well before he got his job and before I got my promotion. Raymond always showed a sincere interest in how we were doing our jobs. He was genuinely curious.

 BARBARA WHITESIDE

I met you when you came to our Skokie, Illinois, store. I was the warehouse manager. I had worked at seven stores in my time working at Service Merchandise, and Skokie was my last store. I remember the day so clearly, as you and I walked the warehouse and you commented on how beautiful my warehouse was. I felt so proud to work for you and your company. Being a female warehouse manager, I had many challenges with others who thought I couldn't do the job—and even a few who tried to sabotage me. Having you comment on my warehouse when I worked so very hard made me so happy. You truly are such a nice and kind person. I feel honored that I got to meet you.

I met my husband working at the Arlington Heights, Illinois, store, and we will be celebrating twenty-five years of marriage this year. We live less than a mile from where the store was. We often talk about the great times at Service Merchandise and all the friends we still have from there.

 LOUIS PICCOLO

Raymond was in town [Queens] on a winter afternoon. He stopped in at store 183, Ozone Park. Once he left 183, Ethiel Melecio called to let me know. A short time later, Raymond arrived at store 116. I greeted him at the front entrance.

He asked, "How long did it take me to get here?"

I said, "Twenty minutes."

He stated that he had never seen this store look so good. He spent some time chatting with jewelry manager Linda Kirkland and me. Raymond congratulated us on our comp sales increase from the prior year.

As he exited, he was blowing kisses to us. Linda and I have maintained regular contact over the years. We still share this story that is so special for us.

I also had the pleasure of meeting him one early morning as he arrived at JFK in New York. His secretary had over-nighted his briefcase to me and asked that I meet him. I met him sometime around four or five in the morning at JFK. After I introduced myself, he asked me jokingly why I was wearing a suit at that hour! I thought it was the right thing to do, and I still believe that. He thanked me profusely— always gracious, respectful, professional.

I would do it all again.

CHAPTER 7

A Love That Endures

DEEP IN MY HEART, the love has endured. Though I no longer was tending to the daily affairs of Service Merchandise, the sense of family that I knew there never faded. Now, as I embarked on a new stage of life, that longtime dedication to the company and its people would continue to sustain me. My love of retail was as strong as ever, and it was time to find new ways to explore it.

Another kind of love was blossoming too. Etta and I had become grandparents. On April 30, 1996, we got word in Nashville that Robyn was going into labor. So at 6:00 a.m., we hopped on a company plane to Boca Raton, Florida, where she and her husband, David, made their home. We got to her hospital room just in time to hear the first wailings from little Sam. He had waited for us to get there. Sam would be followed in three years by Max, and years later Leya would give birth to Ezra and Theo.

Though I stayed on in Nashville a few years as chairman of the board at Service Merchandise, Etta and I were ready to move on. We packed up and headed to Florida in 1999 to be closer to Robyn and David and our grandson, and another on the way. We already had a house in Boca, and for a while it bustled with both our families and two dogs, too, as we waited to move into new houses under construction. It was a joyous time of birth and rebirth, of conclusions and beginnings.

Back to Business

Even before wrapping things up in Nashville, I had learned of a new business opportunity. I was scheduled to attend the Jerry Lewis telethon in Los Angeles, and a couple of my former senior executives asked to meet with me while I was in town. They greeted me at the airport, gifted me a box of chocolate-covered matzo, and asked me to come with them to check out a 99 Cents Only store. They were considering opening similar operations in Nashville.

I joined them on a visit to the store on Wilshire Boulevard. The place was busy, and I noticed a cooler of hot dogs selling for ninety-nine cents for a ten-pack. There were hundreds of packs in that cooler. On a return visit the next day, the cooler was empty. "We sold them all," the assistant manager told me. "And we filled the cooler again. Sold those too." He told me the store had done $10 million in sales for the year.

"Do y'all have more of these stores?" I asked. He told me there were three hundred in the chain, and it was a public company. After I verified the numbers, I had a word with my former colleagues: "If you decide to move to Florida, we'll open some stores like this."

Together we started with three stores that we called 99 Cent Stuff—two in Miami and one in Boynton Beach. Over the next ten years, we built that to eighteen stores. My partners eventually left for other endeavors, and by 2008, not seeing the return I had envisioned, I got out. I'd had a lot of fun buying closeouts and fast-selling items, watching them stack up in the morning and disappear by evening. In all my years at Service Merchandise, I'd been to Asia maybe twice. While running the 99 Cent Stuff stores, I went at least once a year. We did some creative dealing in those stores. In the end, though, what mattered most was that the endeavor be profitable—and it simply wasn't.

So that was my business pursuit during my first decade in Florida. When we first moved there, I played a little golf and a little tennis, but I got a lot more pleasure out of running those stores. I needed retail. It felt great to be back in the game.

WHO'S THE BETTER BUYER?

While I was operating the 99 Cent Stuff stores, I had a buyer whom I entrusted to purchase our hair goods inventory—the barrettes, combs, brushes, and the like. One day I watched as he was choosing items from a salesman. The salesman seemed to smirk at each of the man's choices. After they finished, I asked the salesman if he could hang around a bit longer, and I called our daughter Leya and asked her to stop by the store for a few minutes on her way home from high school.

"Leya, do me a favor," I said when she arrived. "This fellow here has some samples of hair goods. Would you pick out the ones you think would be best for us to carry?"

"Sure," she said, and the salesman smiled at each of her choices. He knew that she was picking just the right stuff. I thanked her, and she went on her way.

I turned to the salesman. "So tell me: who was the better buyer—the guy you usually deal with or my daughter?"

"Oh, your daughter, by far!" he said. I suppose he imagined that I'd be tickled to hear that. Instead, I scowled.

"Why didn't you tell me?" I asked. "You knew he was making the wrong choices for this store, and you just smirked?" The salesman was groping for words. "You should have told me," I repeated. "I trusted you."

He had violated a value that my father had drilled into me so many years before: "Folks will treat you right, Son, if you treat them right." Good advice, yes, on the whole. *But, Daddy, hear me, it doesn't always work out that way.*

A Time for Giving Back

As deep as retail runs in my blood, though, it was far from my only pursuit. I got involved with the United Way in Palm Beach County, serving on the board for a while. I got involved with the Jewish Federation, and I served on the board of Hebrew Union College. For nearly a decade, I was a volunteer at SCORE, which is a large network of business mentors. I found it fulfilling to advise a lot of young people trying to get a business off the ground. It was a way of giving back—because, after all, so many people had helped me along the way. I'm still in touch with some of those entrepreneurs. I'm honored to call them my friends.

During those years, Etta and I were particularly delighted to be involved in an annual Thanksgiving luncheon for older residents who had nowhere else to go for the holiday. Three good friends of ours originated the luncheon, and they eventually gave us and another couple the honor of sponsoring it.

The luncheon is a dress-up affair with entertainment and dancing in the gym of the Jewish Community Center, with restaurant-style table service. For some of the attendees, it was a rare opportunity to socialize and fend off the loneliness that besets so many seniors. For some, it was a reunion. On occasion, the luncheon brought people together who had last seen each other when they were young and living in the same European town or swept into the same concentration camp.

The Jewish Federation and Jewish Family Services helped us to scale up the luncheon so that there was no waiting list. More than seven hundred people attended the latest two that we held, with a robust turnout of community volunteers. During the pandemic years, we helped to rally those volunteers to deliver meals to homes—not quite the same as dressing up for dinner with friends, of course, but it was the same spirit of cooperative service to the community. At family meetings, Etta and I emphasize that if we had to name one thing that we would want continued after we are gone, it would be the Thanksgiving luncheon.

Meanwhile, I continued to serve on the board of Limited Brands, which operated a variety of well-known retail stores. Among them, through the years, were Limited Too, Limited Express, Victoria's

Secret, Bath & Body Works, Abercrombie & Fitch, Cacique, Lane Bryant, Henri Bendel, and Galyan's Trading Company. I served on that board from April of 1984 until May of 2020, and it was a priceless opportunity to learn from superb leadership. During my Service Merchandise years, I was able to implement a lot of that learning, and the experience continued to serve me well through my Florida years.

It was my privilege to represent some of the finest retailing operations in the world.

In a way, serving on that board became my retail lifeline. After the Service stores closed and I got out of the 99 Cent Stuff business, I still had occasion to do something that I enjoy more than golf or cards or most anything else—and that's visiting stores to check out how they are doing. Wherever I roamed—a shopping center, a mall, even downtown London—I could pop in to one of those stores and chat with the employees as a member of the board. I took note of whether I was greeted warmly and swiftly when I entered. I wanted to know what was selling. I checked to see whether the store was well stocked. It was my privilege to represent some of the finest retailing operations in the world.

A PASSION FOR RETAILING

During the thirty-six years that I served on the board of Limited Brands, my love of retail led me to visit the stores quite frequently. I enjoyed those visits immensely. I might be on a layover during a flight, and if one of our stores was in that airport, I would wander in, look around, and ask questions. I was a stickler for inventory. Every store should have every item in stock every day—and I reported any lapses to the top managers.

Whenever I visited a Victoria's Secret store, for example, I would head straight to the bra drawers. I was particularly interested in 32C cups. I knew those were fast sellers, along with the 32Bs, and most likely to be out of stock.

On one visit, as I was busily perusing the bra collection, a saleswoman approached me. "Can I help you, sir?" I looked up, and she was smiling. "Would you be Mr. Zimmerman?" she asked.

"Yes," I said. "I am. How did you know?"

"Well, we've been advised that if a gray-haired gentleman comes into the store and starts poking around in our bra drawers, that's you, probably."

Word gets around. I'm sure the message that the managers intended to hand down to the associates was "Keep a lookout for a gentleman who truly cares about how we're doing." They might not have worded it quite that way, but surely that is what they meant.

Focus on Family

I am deeply grateful for the abundant blessings that have come to our family through the years. Though we cannot reside near all our many loved ones, we travel frequently to visit them—in Tennessee, New York, and California, where my sister Sue lives. Doris passed away in 1989.

Our travels also have taken us to far corners of the world—some places bleak and challenging, and other places progressive and enlightening—where we see how we could join efforts to change people's lives. We witnessed the power of collective action.

We have learned so much about the beauty of other cultures. Among our destinations, to name a few, have been Israel, Ukraine, Moldova, and Russia, as well as China, Morocco, and Turkey.

Our family continues the dedication to community and global responsibility that our parents emphasized. We gather regularly as a family office, making decisions together on finances, investments, goals, and the causes and institutions that we wish to support. We listen carefully to one another's ideas. The emphasis is on family unity. This is why we were honored to sign the Jewish Future Pledge. We embrace the concept of family giving in continuity.

I have never been shy about encouraging others to donate, too, when they have the ability to do so. At times I even made it a requirement of a business deal, though I never have asked anyone to give more than I was willing to give.

Five days a week, I still get up and get dressed and head to my office—and it's away from the house, not in some spare room. I am not "working," mind you, but I'm doing daily those things that others call work. Such is "retirement." One must remain active. I attend to family office matters, and I keep in touch with the Service Merchandise family, which has never ceased to mean so much to me. Once a week on Wednesdays, I have lunch with Etta's father, Alex Gross, who is just a few years my senior. I know he will always want to make sure that I am taking good care of his daughter.

I have not mentioned many people by name in this book, and that is by design. To include all who have meant so much to me and who have contributed richly to a lifetime of memories would add a hundred pages—and still the odds are that I would overlook someone. Nonetheless, I must single out a few right now because, well, they are among the people I love most:

Our children: Fred, Robyn, and Leya. We are supremely proud of each of them. Fred has held prominent leadership positions in Jewish and philanthropic initiatives in his community as well as nationally and globally. He is the quiet giant with an intense sense of humor. He and Etta often have traveled together worldwide on many missions to communities in distress. In many ways, Fred is a force of good for anyone in his life. Robyn, too, has been devoted to philanthropic work, and she is active in her synagogue. After moving to Florida, she established two businesses, and she took a position as a consultant for a nonprofit. And did I say she's a wonderful mom? So is Leya, who with her husband, Joel, has added two new grandsons to our family. After college, she began a career in New York City, eventually working in high-end fashion marketing and sales. Most recently, she has been head of all sales for a digital marketing company. She has integrity and a strong work ethic, as do all our children, and I am pleased that I had the opportunity to help instill that value and that I could be their cheerleader.

Our grandchildren. Sam and Max are now in their twenties. On Thanksgiving weekend of 2020, Sam married Jordyn—our first granddaughter-in-law! In recent years we became grandparents anew when Leya became a mom. Ezra was born in 2018, and Theo in 2021. As Pawpaw and Mammaw, we delighted in our new roles. I so vividly recall time spent with the boys at their various ball games—even soccer, a sport that I find less than interesting. (Max once declared, "I love Pawpaw the most because I don't play soccer.") They came with me regularly on food deliveries to a retirement community. We have lately included Sam and Max in our family office discussions, and I haven't the slightest doubt they will be joined one day by Ezra and Theo and others yet to come.

My dearest Etta. By now, dear reader, I am sure you have gathered that I am seldom at a loss for words. My mouth has a way of going into overdrive before I stop to think—but now, as I think of all that my wife has meant to me, no words seem adequate to express how I feel. It's something like awe. Etta has a heart that embraces her community, by which I mean our world. In dozens of trips to Eastern Europe, she has dedicated herself to relief work with the American Jewish Joint Distribution Committee. She has served as president and board chairman of the local Jewish Federation. And in her work with the PJ Library, she has done so much to instill our culture and faith in the coming generations. For that I praise her—but it is her influence on our family and how she has kept us together that leaves me speechless. I confess I'm not easy to live with. When I don't think to do the things that I should, Etta does the thinking for me. She encourages, counsels, and motivates me. Truly, were it not for her, I would not be alive now to write these words. Ours is a love for all time.

Postscript

In 1961, after committing ourselves to the catalog business, we proudly dressed up our original warehouse at 305 Broadway in Nashville with aluminum siding and displayed the bold lettering of our new name: *Service Merchandise*. Thirty-six years later, we leased the building to a restaurant that occupied the site for a time. The restaurant people, in their remodeling, tore down that aluminum siding—and there, emblazoned on the old front window, were the words *Service Wholesale Company*, our identity from once upon a time. It felt like the opening of a time capsule.

At that point, many of our stores were closing, and within five years they all were gone. "We need to buy the name," Etta told me in 2002, the year that Service Merchandise liquidated. I saw her point clearly. Inherent in our company name was the brand that we had nurtured all those years—our history, our mission, our spirit. How unfair to our loyal customers and employees—to our Service Merchandise family—if someone else were to grab the rights to that name and abuse it for their own gain.

We had no immediate plans to do anything with the name other than to safeguard its dignity and integrity. Eventually, though, starting in 2004, we set up a website offering online sales. Sometimes people have clicked on it to ask for the replacement battery they were promised when they bought a watch years ago. Or to ask for the latest catalog. Or they ask where they might find one of the hundreds of thousands of Christmas bells that we once included with every purchase.

Some folks think we're still a brick-and-mortar business, though the last store closed twenty years ago. "Our stores are all closed," I explain, but they insist they saw one. And they did—or, rather, what once was one of our stores. A couple of the old buildings, closed for two decades, still sport the company name in big letters for all to see, at least as recently as a few years ago.

Though our online site hasn't consistently been active, Leya has recently relaunched it. It's a joy to know that as I write the final words to this book, the Service Merchandise name endures.

We also have an online presence today on private Facebook pages where our Service Merchandise family—the associates, customers, vendors, and everyone else who made us what we were—swap memories of our time together. I log on now and then to remember and to smile. Across the nation, smaller social media groups also have formed, all of them dedicated to their experiences in our stores. Former colleagues still stay in touch with one another. They even gather for reunions.

I have visited twenty-three such sites, adding numerous names to my roster of about five thousand people so far to whom I send cards by email each year to celebrate birthdays and anniversaries. And every year, at least a fifth of them write back to me. In the days before email, I signed each greeting that went out. At business meetings, the first thing I would take from my briefcase would be the

About half a million people worked for Service Merchandise at one time or another.

day's cards to sign, which I did without missing a word being said. I felt that an important part of my job was the personal touch. I still do. I estimate that about half a million people worked for Service Merchandise at one time or another—and I can tell you, if it were humanly possible, I would send out half a million cards.

I am delighted to keep in touch with my Service Merchandise family. I recently shared some wonderful news with those on my email list, virtually all of whom participated in some way in our annual

MDA campaigns. Newly approved drugs have been able to halt the progression of the muscle disease, offering life-changing hope for many families. The response to that news was powerful. They were excited to have been part of a great effort to improve lives.

Some of those who post online recall their days working at a first job where they learned the values of teamwork. Others built careers with us and went on to success in their own businesses. A few fell in love with the young man or young woman at the other end of the counter who became their partner in life. Some came just for a summer and left with dollars in their pocket and friends for a lifetime. We were together then, all of us younger, living and laughing and sharing something special. And in our memories, we are together still.

ABOUT THE AUTHOR

Raymond Zimmerman cofounded the retail giant Service Merchandise with his parents in 1960. He became CEO in 1983 and served in that capacity until retiring in April 1997. He grew the company from its initial store in Nashville, Tennessee, to a bustling retail chain of over four hundred catalog showroom stores. Raymond retired and relocated to Florida in 1999. He founded discount retailer 99 Cent Stuff and operated those stores from 1999 to 2008.

Raymond proudly served as a director on the L Brands' board from 1984 to 2021. He has served as a lecturer and mentor to those interested in retailing and entrepreneurial endeavors. Concurrent with his business obligations, he has always been engaged in bettering his community. He was the recipient of the Alexis de Tocqueville Society Award for the United Way of Middle Tennessee. He took active leadership roles in United Way of America, the Muscular Dystrophy Association, and the Jewish Federations of his two hometowns of Nashville and Boca Raton, respectively.

Raymond is married to Etta Zimmerman, and he is the proud father to Fred Zimmerman, Robyn Rubinoff, and Leya Kaufman. He also is thrilled to have four grandsons.

CPSIA information can be obtained
at www.ICGtesting.com
Printed in the USA
BVHW091907211022
649988BV00003B/125

9 781642 252842